YOU CAN GET MORE REST
FROM LESS SLEEP . . .

- Shorter sleep may be positive
- Quality sleep makes quantity less important
- Regularity is necessary for efficient sleep
- Deep sleep is essential for physical health
- Many creative people need little sleep

Sleep is one of life's mysteries. In this bold new book, Everett Mattlin explores why we sleep and what we can do to get more rest out of fewer hours. If you're one of those people who's always wishing there were more hours in the day, you owe it to yourself to read this book.

Sleep Less, Live More

Everett Mattlin

BALLANTINE BOOKS • NEW YORK

Library of Congress Catalog Card Number: 79-2593

ISBN 0-345-29037-2

This edition published by arrangement with
J. B. Lippincott Company

Manufactured in the United States of America

First Ballantine Books Edition: November 1980

For Barbara, with love

CONTENTS

FOREWORD

The current concept of sleep is in the process of change. Modern sleep laboratories, sleep centers and sleep clinics specializing in the study of sleep difficulties have not quelled the controversy regarding this important human activity. For all our advanced technology and scientific investigations, no "normal" sleep time has been established. No one really knows what sleep is, what purpose it serves or if it is really necessary. The sleep state is a unique, highly personalized condition that varies in the same individual at different times, depending on existing mental and physical needs. It is also recognized that, in certain stages, sleep is not as restful as it was once thought to be. In fact, it can be highly anxiety-provoking. Recuperative sleep work or dream work is also not as significant as was formerly thought.

The need for sleep, once considered a basic instinct, is being questioned. Instincts are survival drives, yet some people have been observed to be able to survive on little or no sleep with no apparent permanent traumatic sequelae to body or mind. Clinical evidence seems to imply that it is not the quantity of sleep but its quality that is restful and restorative.

Since the need for sleep is questionable, whether instinctual or learned, and since investigations into sleep reduction have shown no deleterious effects on physical or mental functioning, an interesting question presents itself: Why not develop the habit of sleeping less so that more waking time is available for constructive use?

Everett Mattlin describes an easily learned behavior modification technique for sensible sleep reduction. It is worth noting that he refers to sleep reduction, not sleep deprivation. Psychologically, the latter term invites negative images; the author, however, is reassuring in his message that not only sleeping less but sleeplessness itself is not necessarily hazardous to one's health. In fact—contrary to popular opinion—it can be quite beneficial at times. Throughout it is suggested that the reader try to follow the book's philosophy: Take a chance and learn how to sleep less. You just might enjoy it more. After all, there is nothing to lose except a little sleep.

Abraham Weinberg, M.D.

Co-founder, the Sleep and Somatic Therapy Center and the Morton Prince Clinic for Hypnotherapy

New York
June 1979

ACKNOWLEDGMENTS

Of course, I found the published studies of the country's leading sleep experts invaluable, but I also discovered that these experts could be generous of time and gracious in spirit in response to personal inquiries. My special thanks to Drs. Peter Hauri of Dartmouth, Wilse B. Webb of the University of Florida, Laverne C. Johnson of the Naval Health Research Center in San Diego and Frederick J. Evans of the University of Pennsylvania. Special thanks, too, to my editor, Kathryn Frank, who helped hone the message of this book with integrity and skill. My appreciation, as well, to Eva Zelig and Doris Howard, who assisted in the book's preparation.

INTRODUCTION

Think of it: when was the last time you wished there were more hours in the day? Chances are it was yesterday, even today, for—given the cares and complexities of most of our lives—it's certainly one of the most pressing wishes of our hectic world. Inevitably, we all try to cut down on our lists of Things to Do, but it's simply no use. What with work that spills over into our evenings and weekends, our families, our friends, our various commitments to home and community, life is fraught with conflicting and time-consuming demands. And even if we apply the latest techniques for wisely managing time and ordering priorities, there still don't seem to be enough hours in the day to get it all done, much less reward us with spare time for ourselves. What we all really need, it would seem, is a day stretcher.

If that sounds fanciful, consider how often you've thought carefully about one solution. If you could sleep just one hour less than you've been sleeping, you could gain a measure of peace and quiet in the morning to clear up matters at the office or at home, or some time in the evening to read that long neglected book, pursue a new interest, polish an old one. With two extra hours a day, perhaps you could swing both. All very promising, until you remember how tired and ineffectual you may have felt at times when you went through a period of days when your night's sleep was significantly reduced. You seem to *need* your sleep.

Of course you do. We all do. But maybe not as

much as we think. Sleep research, however sophisticated, is a fairly new field and has thus far left a great many questions unanswered. But it has certainly cast doubt on the question of how much sleep we really need to survive and thrive, and some very recent studies suggest that almost all of us can cut back on our sleep—within limits, of course—without impairing our health or proficiency. In fact, we are likely to perform and feel better.

This book will show you how to go about it. It will explore what is known about sleep and the amount our bodies and minds really need. It will free you of the compulsive conviction that you can't function without seven or eight hours of sleep. We'll visit sleep research laboratories, review studies in professional journals, hear what physicians, psychiatrists and psychologists specializing in sleep research and therapy have to say on the subject and look at actual sleep reduction experiments conducted in government and university-sponsored programs. We'll examine ways of improving the quality of our sleep, which can help us curb the quantity we need. And, finally, we'll learn how to stretch the day by following a carefully delineated program that offers a medically validated, safe, commonsense approach to sleep reduction.

Habits of a lifetime take time to change, which explains why most of us experience difficulties after a night or two of abbreviated sleep. Keeping this in mind, the program outlined in this book introduces a step-by-step reduction schedule that allows you time to adjust gradually to a new routine and make it an ongoing pattern in your life. The program prescribes no pills, medication, self-hypnosis or gimmicks. In fact, all you really need to bring to it is the genuine desire to sleep less so that you can accomplish more with your new-found waking hours.

And motivation *does* make the difference. After all,

sleep is definitely one of life's greatest pleasures. You won't want to leave your bed earlier in the morning if there's no compelling reason, and it will continue to lure you back at night if you have nothing better to do. We all know what a difference motivation makes in our attitude toward sleep. When we're off on a vacation trip, we don't mind bounding out of bed before sunup, and if there's a good film on television or a book we want to finish, we don't seem to notice if we sacrifice sleep that night. When we're with friends we like we can talk until two in the morning, while at a dinner party with people we don't care for we often find our lids growing heavy by the time dessert is served. We can be studying for an exam and fighting sleep when someone suggests going out for a pizza and a beer and our revival is miraculous. Obviously, all the time in the world is not going to keep us awake if we're not using it for what we really want to do.

This simple but critical point is affirmed by Dr. Nathaniel Kleitman, Professor Emeritus of the University of Chicago and the dean of sleep researchers; as a matter of fact, it was in his laboratories that modern sleep research really began. When asked about the possibility of shortening one's sleep hours, he was very direct: "You *can* train yourself to change, just the way a dieter forces himself to eat less. People do it. What do women do, for example, when they have kids? But you have to want to, to have something to be awake for. There has to be a reason to stay awake. I put it in terms not of how much sleep you need, but of your wakefulness capability—how long you can be awake. If you have the incentive, the curiosity to be awake, then you'll stay awake and sleep less as a result."[1]

In fact, someone undertaking a sleep reduction plan soon realizes that it's impossible to divorce sleep from the rest of his or her life. If we don't feel well, of course we want to be in bed longer, and it's also true that if we're upset mentally, or even plain bored, that pillow is magnetic. It's an aspect of sleep that has particularly intrigued Dr. Ernest Hartmann, a psychiatrist who is also a professor at Tufts University and head of the sleep laboratory at Boston State Hospital. He has found that stress and anxiety make people want to sleep more and that those who are calm and integrated seem to need less sleep. Though not all sleep experts agree with him, he is convinced that short sleepers are more energetic, confident, successful and happier people.[2] We speak of "sleepy" personalities and "wide-awake" personalities, and there is some commonsense truth in those descriptions: anyone wanting to go, do, achieve, gather in experience resents hours lost in sleep.

This must be true of you, since you're reading this book. And you'll find that following its sleep reduction program, in itself, will help you gain a new command over your life. The very first week you sleep less you gain precious extra hours, and what you accomplish with that time gives you fresh impetus to push on. Soon your goals expand as you reach previous ones, daily reinforcing your self-confidence and motivation. Parallel attitudes toward self-improvement begin to develop: you'll find that your newfound sense of control, the improved efficiency of your life and your recognition of its growing potential motivate improved eating habits, daily exercise, even the elimination of cigarettes and other such dramatic fitness measures. The chain of influence builds along with the quantum leaps in your incentive. You start to enjoy a far more positive approach to career and personal fulfillment as old yearnings turn into realities. That's why a sleep reduction effort can be an excellent catalyst to help you take charge of your life and work toward becoming the kind of person you want to be.

I am particularly aware of the benefits that can be won because I've personally experienced them. I undertook the program offered here, with every bit of the skepticism you're no doubt bringing to your reading. Given my long years of entrenched sleep habits, I was quite certain I'd collapse entirely if I didn't get my necessary eight hours of sleep—and beyond that, I had serious doubts about the medical advisability of curtailing my sleep. Careful research quelled my reservations about the effects on my health, and within approximately five months I cut back from eight hours to six, finding that I had gained not only new vitality but also dramatically boosted ambition and optimism about the direction of my life.

There's an outside chance that you'll find that you can't succeed with this program, that you're someone who simply must have eight hours of sleep—whatever the reasons. But you won't know without trying, and the potential rewards should convince you to make a determined effort. Remember that the doctors who have conducted experiments in sleep reduction believe that most people *can* succeed—that they can cut back on sleep time without being sleepy, without any harm to health or psyche or ability to perform.

Cut back by how much? For most eight-hour sleepers, an hour to two hours is a reasonable expectation. More may be possible for those who want to push harder. But even an additional half hour a day would be welcome to most of us, and in an extra hour you could indeed clear your desk or learn French or take up the piano or pursue some other hobby or skill you've long thought about. One and a half hours a day would give you an additional 547 hours a year, the equivalent of an extra month of waking hours.

That's like adding a year to every twelve years you will live. Sleep two hours less and you add a year to every nine.

You can claim that extra time. As Dr. Kleitman suggested, reducing sleep is in a way like going on a diet, and you can consider this book, if you wish, as offering a "sleep diet" plan. Like ordinary dieting, sleep dieting takes motivation and willpower. But you will end up achieving more, feeling better about yourself and glad about the day you decided to trim that sleep fat off your life forever.

CHAPTER 1
Sleep Length: There Is No Norm

"Eight hours for work, eight hours for play, and eight hours for sleep."
   Alfred the Great, ninth-century Saxon king (also ascribed to Maimonides, twelfth-century philosopher)

"5:00: Rise, wash . . . 10:00: Sleep."
   Benjamin Franklin, *Autobiography*

"And yet a third of life is passed in sleep."
   Lord Byron, *Don Juan*

Seven to eight hours of sleep would seem to be an inherited need of mankind. We've been conditioned, generation after generation, to think that without this span of restorative unconsciousness, our bodies and our minds will suffer. Whether or not we've heard about circadian rhythms and biological clocks, we suspect that ignoring conventional sleep timing is an affront to nature. And if we don't pay for lost sleep today, it will come and haunt us tomorrow.

Our parents, of course, have contributed to these attributes, drumming into our heads that "lots of sleep is good for you," administering it as a kind of instant cure for tiredness after a busy day, for peevishness or for the first sneeze or cough of a cold. Naturally, we were all too young to realize a distinct possibility: that the great majority of us were perhaps being trained in

1

childhood to sleep longer than we needed, simply because of the natural desire of our parents to get us out of their hair and into bed. In any event, we were instilled at an early age with the mystique and power of sleep. Lose some of it and we felt both guilty (because we'd disobeyed universal law) and frightened by the threat of becoming ill or nonfunctional.

Our family doctors have most likely reinforced these beliefs. A large part of the medical profession seems to accept the dictum that we need seven to eight hours of sleep as part of a healthy regimen. In 1978 both the American Medical Association and Blue Cross/Blue Shield ran advertisements in magazines and newspapers across the country heralding seven rules for maintaining health. Along with the need for adequate exercise and the avoidance of cigarettes, the list included an admonition to "get seven to eight hours of sleep every day." If you sent for the insurance group's booklet, you found this elaboration: "Doctors tell us we need about seven hours a night from twenty to fifty-five years of age, slightly less when older."[1]

Supporting this medical opinion is the fact that most people do indeed seem to sleep for seven to eight hours. The Department of Commerce, for example, recently disclosed the results of a survey of "use of time by city dwellers," and average sleep time came out to 7.8 hours a night.[2] There have been other surveys, but the most ambitious was conducted by the Gallup Poll in the United States, Canada, Great Britain, France, the Netherlands, Denmark, Norway and Sweden, and it pegged the average at seven and a half hours.[3] That average holds within the same seven- to eight-hour range even among the Eskimos of Northern Canada and Alaska, who sleep as long as we do during their long-night winters and short-night summers.[4] On one expedition to the Arctic in the 1950s the men were told they could sleep as long as they liked but to keep a record of their sleep schedule: there was little variation month to month, in spite of the difference in the light and darkness circle, and the average sleep time came out to 7.9 hours.[5]

It's hardly surprising, then, that most of us not only sleep seven to eight hours but are also convinced that we need that amount to survive in our pressurized world. After all, if the practice is so widespread, there must be something inherently necessary about it. And so pervasive is the notion that we need at least those seven hours in bed that many of us who do get by on fewer hours are also worried. Special clinics that treat insomnia and other sleep problems report they are frequently consulted by people who are concerned about their health because they seem to need only five or six hours of sleep to feel perfectly rested.

The Eight-Hour Myth

The doctors at those clinics—who specialize in sleep disorders and therefore know a good deal more about sleep needs than most general practitioners—simply tell such persons to go home and stop worrying. They're perfectly normal. In fact, they're lucky. Yes, seven to eight hours of sleep is indeed the world's average, but they just happen to need less than the average. "Average," after all, means that many people sleep more than eight hours or less than seven, and doctors have failed to discover any health deficit anywhere along the spectrum. When Dr. Wilse B. Webb of the University of Florida, one of the world's leading authorities on sleep, saw the AMA and Blue Cross/ Blue Shield ads, he was upset: "They are throwing us back five years—no, ten years. They're wholly incorrect and condemning roughly sixty percent of the population who get less or more sleep to needless worry. If your book does nothing else, at least it can counter that myth." Dr. Webb once felt strongly enough about the issue to write an article for *The New York Times* in which he said, "One of the most pervasive and mischievous myths about sleep is that everyone needs eight hours of sleep per night. . . . Unfortunately, it seems to be human nature to turn the average into a norm or target to achieve."[6]

Dr. William C. Dement, a pioneer in the field of sleep research who now heads the country's largest sleep disorders clinic at Stanford, calls the statement that everyone needs eight hours of sleep a "fallacy" that is a throwback to the rules in hygiene books of a generation ago (and truly productive sleep research, which has challenged many time-honored notions about sleep, is only a generation old).[7] Dr. Kleitman, who has taken particular delight over the years in puncturing myths about sleep, says flatly, "There is no more a 'normal' duration of sleep, for either children or adults, than there is a normal heart rate, or height, or weight. Comparison with composite values may tell an individual whether his particular figure is close to or far removed from the mean, but in most cases attempts to reach that mean are either impossible, unnecessary or both."[8]

What these preeminent authorities in the sleep research field are saying is that *there's simply no official, certified number of hours of sleep we must abide by in order not to endanger our well-being.* Instead, there is great diversity in sleep patterns, a diversity that is as normal as human diversity in height and hair coloring or in the size of the hats or shoes we wear.

Sleep Patterns Vary, from Cradle to Grave

It's a diversity, moreover, that starts with birth and persists throughout life. Records show that some newborn infants sleep less than eleven hours and others sleep as many as twenty-two. In the first six months of life, it's not unusual for one baby to average twelve hours and another sixteen. About fifty percent of babies sleep through the night at two months, while the other half—as their parents know only too well—do not.[9] Since these are all perfectly healthy babies, we have to conclude that wide variations in sleep patterns exist from the very beginning of life.

At the age of two, the average sleep time, including naps, is a little over twelve hours and by the age of five it has come down to about eleven. Then from six to the late teens there is a gradual reduction from eleven to the sleep patterns of adulthood. But, again, those are only averages. Actual practice varies widely, and sleep experts tell parents who worry that their children aren't getting the "proper" amount of sleep to stop worrying and let up on the kids. "Many two-year-old children need less sleep than most ten-year-old children," says Dr. Peter Hauri, head of Dartmouth's sleep clinic.[10] Children tend to find their own comfort level and will nap or go to bed earlier if they get sleepy—though, of course, parents have to watch to see that they aren't forcing themselves to stay up even when they *are* sleepy. Many children are made miserable by parents who force them to follow strict, arbitrary sleep rules.

At about the age of eighteen to twenty, people usually establish the sleep pattern they will follow at least until middle age—whether it be nine, eight or seven hours or less. A conservative estimate would be that about half of all adults sleep seven to eight hours and twenty percent sleep more than eight hours—which still leaves about one out of every three persons who averages less than seven hours a night. Of course, there's no way of knowing whether this ratio has been constant over the centuries, but at least some evidence exists that there's always been an observable proportion of the population that didn't believe nature demands seven or eight hours of sleep from us. The British jurist Sir Edward Coke wrote this epigram about sleep back in Queen Elizabeth I's day:

Six hours in sleep, in law's grave study six,
Four hours spend in prayer, the rest on Nature fix.

And two old anonymous sayings about sleep suggest again that eight hours were never universally assumed to be necessary: "Six hours for a man, seven for a woman, eight hours for a fool" and "Nature requires five, custom takes seven, laziness nine and wickedness eleven."

We all know that older people, as the Blue Cross/ Blue Shield booklet suggested, need less sleep. Isn't it odd that persons past sixty, seventy or eighty—who tire so easily that you would guess they need *more* sleep to stay healthy—sleep *less* on an average? The average sleep time after sixty drops to about six and a half hours.[11]

But again, that, too, is only an average. Variability in our sleep habits increases tremendously as we grow older: some old people who once slept seven to eight hours will start to sleep five hours, and others, counting their daytime naps, will sleep eleven. Dr. Webb suggests that the reason for the increased variability may lie in the fact that centuries ago people didn't even live beyond the age of thirty or forty, and so sleep patterns in old age aren't as fixed over as many years.

Many Lucky People Are "Natural Short Sleepers"

The range in the length of sleep of under-sixty adults is also quite amazing. Some regularly sleep nine and ten hours. Many people—perhaps twenty to twenty-five percent of us—get by nicely on six to seven hours, and maybe five percent sleep between five and six hours. Some persons—probably fewer than one in a hundred—seem to need even less. And we aren't referring to people who suffer from insomnia or who sleep four or five hours a night for a few nights when they are finishing a term paper or starting a love affair, but to those who sleep only a few hours night after night all their adult lives. They want and seem to need no more: they wake up as fresh from their four or four and a half hours of sleep as those who get twice that amount. And they are just as healthy in mind and body.

Dr. Hauri, for example, examined a seventy-one-year-old woman whose husband felt there must be something wrong with her, for she was sleeping less than four hours a night. The woman herself wasn't complaining: she felt fine. She hiked in the summer and went cross-country skiing every day in the winter. Dr. Hauri tested her and proclaimed her "sound as a bell."[12]

Dr. Dement tells of a late colleague, Professor B. Q. Morgan, who had been chairman of Stanford's German department. At the age of twenty-three, on a trip to Germany, he went to bed at 10:00 P.M. and woke up at 2:00 A.M. and couldn't get to sleep again. Four hours became his sleep pattern for the rest of his life. In his eightieth year, the professor slept in Dement's lab for five nights and proved that four hours' sleep was all he "needed."[13]

We know that many of history's most dynamic leaders have been short sleepers—Frederick the Great and the Duke of Wellington, for example, and Napoleon, who needed only three to four hours of sleep. Certainly many American presidents have been short sleepers—Lyndon Johnson most markedly in recent history, who would work past midnight and function energetically on just four to five hours of sleep including an afternoon nap.[14] Harry Truman and John F. Kennedy also knew how to get by on less sleep by supplementing night sleep with short naps. And according to his personal physician, Dr. William Lukash, President Carter usually goes to bed after the eleven o'clock news and is up in time to settle down to work at 6:00 A.M.[15] In crisis periods he will get even less sleep. During the intensive Middle East peace negotiations at Camp David with President Sadat and Prime Minister Begin in 1978, the President hardly slept at all; he subsisted on short naps.[16]

Cabinet members, other top U.S. officials and legislators grapple with almost equally demanding agendas and schedules. Secretary of Labor Ray Marshall, for example, says he normally sleeps five hours, and that has been true all his adult life, long before he entered public office. Now, he says, "sometimes I get less than five." (*The Wall Street Journal* once reported that on the road he often gets only three and a half.[17]) Marshall says he wakes up in the morning feeling refreshed and ready to tackle the day's work. He adds, though, that dull work can make him nod, "and I therefore do it first."

One U.S. Senator who is a short sleeper is Patrick Leahy, the junior senator from Vermont. He says he wakes up feeling totally refreshed after only four or five hours of sleep. Occasionally he'll take a twenty-minute nap during the afternoon, but in that case he may sleep only three hours the following night. He is only thirty-eight now, but he says his sleep requirement just keeps going down. "At my present rate," he jokes, "I may stay awake forever once I turn sixty."

New York's popular mayor Edward Koch, another dynamic political figure whose post is claimed by many to be the second most demanding in the United States, is also a short sleeper. He said in a television interview that he doesn't get to bed until 12:30 or 1:00 A.M. and that he is usually up by 6:00 A.M. "I open up City Hall."

Political and military leaders, men and women of action, are not the only short sleepers. Many creative thinkers and artistic geniuses have needed little sleep: Virgil, Horace, Darwin, Spencer and George Bernard

Shaw have been so identified. Shaw always went to bed well after midnight and was up at 6:00 A.M.

The best known short sleeper in history is probably Thomas Edison. This amazingly prolific inventor often spoke disparagingly of sleep as a colossal waste of time. Indeed, his comments sometimes give the impression that he didn't sleep at all, that he subsisted instead on a couple of ten-minute naps a day. Well, that isn't true, for from the reminiscences of those who worked with him and his own statements to interviewers, we know that Edison actually averaged about four hours of sleep a day—and an hour or so more later in life. But his schedule was wildly irregular. Once deeply engrossed in a project, he would indeed go without sleep for as long as five days, after which he would sleep eighteen or twenty-four hours straight. He would also work through much of the night and then collapse on a worktable, with a couple of books for a pillow, for a long nap. But he certainly resented every hour of sleep that took him away from his work.[18]

Super-Achievers Are Often Short Sleepers

As for well-known contemporary figures, there are numerous examples of short sleepers. Television announcer Ed McMahon of the Johnny Carson show needs only four or five hours a night. Academy Award–winning actress Cloris Leachman once told Carson on the show that she sleeps only *three* hours a night because there are so many things she wants to do. Jackie Gleason's sleep need has been four to five hours most of his life. "I can't explain it, but it's all I require," his personal publicity man remembers him saying. John Weitz, the fashion designer, says he's been a lifelong five-hour sleeper: "If I slept eight hours, I'd just feel I'd wasted time." Drama and dance critic Clive Barnes is another five-hour sleeper. Brendan Gill, the *New Yorker* writer and critic, says that "four hours is about enough for me." George Plimpton is another writer who needs little sleep and told Francesco Scavullo— reported in Scavullo's book, *On Men*—"I think people sleep too long."

Isaac Asimov would agree. Asimov is one of the most prolific writers of this or any time, having published 201 books to date. He's written science fiction, of course, but also children's books, poetry, literary criticism and books on subjects ranging from the Bible to Shakespeare. He lectures widely, writes magazine articles and edits a science fiction magazine. One major reason Asimov gets so much done, he claims, is that he has slept only five to six hours a night since adolescence. He wakes up at 5:00 or 6:00 A.M., "completely ready to go," and works through till 8:00, often to 10:00 P.M. "I hate sleep," he says. "It wastes time."

Not all short sleepers are celebrities, of course. There are short sleepers all around you—your friends, the people you work with. If you aren't aware of them, it's because sleep is a very private matter and often they don't talk about it. They know that many people consider seven to eight hours of sleep "normal" and that if they confess they sleep only four hours they will be put down as "abnormal." But they're out there. Consider:

A fellow in his mid-twenties and in medical school who averages four hours of sleep each night and has time for reading outside his specialty. A man in his forties who works in publishing and who has been sleeping four hours for as long as he can remember. ("Sure, it's helped my career," he says. "Geniuses are rare, you know, so if you work twice as hard—unless you're really stupid—you're bound to get ahead.") A woman in corporate communications who says she has always been a four-hour sleeper, wakes up "peppy" and in good spirits and uses her extra time to jog, play the guitar, make pottery, paint, read and help the handicapped with occupational therapy. A middle-aged man who sleeps about four hours and uses his extra time to pursue a host of interests—raising orchids ("I was in the greenhouse a quarter after five this morning"), coin collecting, cooking, tennis, swimming, fishing, reading. And we've all met many, many more people like them.

Some People Need Even Less Than Four Hours

Is four hours the irreducible minimum amount of sleep people need to not only survive but thrive? It does seem to be the minimum length with which an appreciable number of people are comfortable. Dr. Ray Meddis, a British sleep authority who deplores what he calls "misleading pronouncements from the medical profession concerning 'normal' amounts of sleep," says, "A lot of suffering would disappear overnight if people could be convinced that we 'need' only four hours' sleep and the rest is luxury."[19]

But there are instances of people who do beautifully with even less sleep than that. The first published reports concerning such persons whose stories were verified by serious researchers appeared about ten years ago. Henry Jones, an Australian doctor, and Ian Oswald, a respected Scottish sleep researcher, published an article about two Australian men who slept less than three hours a night.[20] During a week spent in a laboratory, one man, fifty-four years old, slept an average of two hours and forty-seven minutes; the other, aged thirty, averaged a few minutes less. They were monitored, tested and examined, and proved to be busy, healthy, successful men who simply felt no need for more sleep. The younger of the two, a drafts-

man, said he had decided some six years earlier that
his work, his church and his volunteer hours with youth
organizations meant more to him than seven hours in
bed and that was that.

Well, here was pretty good evidence that humans—
at least two among us—could get by with less than
three hours of sleep. Could anyone beat that? Dr. Meddis decided to find out. He let the press know that he
was looking for a person who slept fewer than three
hours—two, say, or maybe less. After a few discour-
aging false leads, Meddis found a woman who has
since achieved considerable fame in sleep literature.
She was then seventy years old, a retired nurse, a
cheerful soul who reported that there's so much to be
done in this world that she hadn't bothered to sleep
more than an hour since childhood. She was invited
to the laboratory.

The first night she said she was too excited by the
experience to sleep at all. She just chatted with the
researchers. The second night, ditto. The third night
she was persuaded to try to get a little shut-eye. She
managed about an hour and a half.

Meddis, elated by his find, asked her to come back
to his lab, this time for five nights, for further corrob-
oration. He had her chaperoned, for example, to
make sure she took no unreported naps. For the five
nights she averaged sixty-seven minutes of sleep a
night, which disappointed her a bit because her own
two-week sleep log, kept earlier at Meddis's request,
had shown an average of only forty-nine minutes. She
was an admirable woman of robust personality and
splendid energy. She used her long, long days to tend
sick friends, to do community work, to write and paint
and read and crochet. She never felt drowsy or in need
of more sleep. At night she would usually read, falling
asleep about 2:00 A.M. with the book in her hand,
and wake up about an hour later, refreshed and ready
to be active again.[21]

Other super-short sleepers have appeared since then —a twenty-five-year-old man who sleeps less than two hours a day who was checked out in a laboratory in Canada, for example.[22] There are even reports from time to time of people who get by on no sleep at all. In the 1930s stories circulated about an old woman in the Bengal jungle who rarely, if ever, closed her eyes. Then there was a yogi in India who hadn't slept—or eaten anything—in twenty-five years.[23] And more recently one Luigi Mario Valsania from a small town in Italy had considerable publicity. A retired farmer, he claimed he went to an all-night party in 1947 and found he couldn't fall asleep after it or ever again.[24] Unfortunately, we don't know if there's any truth to his story, for sleep researchers were skeptical and never invited him to their labs for testing. The experts say that we all need at least some sleep, even if it's only one hour. And if people aren't sleeping at all, it's because they are suffering organic brain damage and are about to pass over into the sleep that's eternal.

But it's fascinating, is it not, that some people sleep only four or three or two or even only one hour a night and feel the need for no more? They certainly should dispel once and for all any notion that human beings need at least seven hours of sleep to function and stay well.

Can We Change Our Sleep Habits?

Why do some people "need" so much less sleep than others? No one really knows for certain. Inheritance is a large—perhaps the prime—factor in determining our sleep patterns; short sleepers, for example, tend to run in families. Nutrition, illness and one's general physical environment in early years also have an effect. We're certainly influenced, too, by the way we've been brought up. As Dr. Webb says, "It is not hard to believe that two children brought up to believe and . . . conform to a pattern that implied in one case that sleep was 'vital' and in the other that it was 'wasteful' would exhibit opposite sleep patterns."[25] Dr. Abraham Weinberg, who treats sleep disorders in New York City, is convinced that one reason we think we need eight hours of sleep is that our parents told us so in order to get us out of the way in the evening. "A sleeping baby means a free parent."[26]

But for whatever reason—heredity or upbringing or both—we all seem to have our own sleep "need." And if you don't know yours, you can discover it by going to bed every night at the same time for a week and waking up without an alarm clock. Most people, however, can tell you what they think their need is without any such experiment: "I've got to get my eight hours or I'm worthless" or "Six, six and a half, something like that, does just fine for me."

The question then is, how much flexibility do we have? Is that need narrowly defined and sacrosanct, or can we change it, and if so, how much and by what means? Specifically, can short sleepers be made as well as born? We'll be searching for detailed answers in this book, but basically the evidence shows that we *can* alter our present sleep patterns—within limits. Few will be able to cut back from eight hours to four—though it has been done—but most people can sleep an hour or two less than they do now and feel just as rested and restored. We'll explore later how it can be done.

But just consider now the fact that some people who must cut back on their sleep for extended periods usually manage very well. One prime example is the medical intern whose hours of duty in a hospital require him to overturn his old sleep habits completely. One doctor, who had been a "long" sleeper—nine hours a night, even ten—recalls the misery of his internship, when he averaged four or five hours of sleep and was "literally bouncing off the walls." But, to his own amazement, in about three months he adjusted and felt just fine.

Of course, interns have no choice, but legions of people have reduced their sleep time just because they wanted to. Usually the process is gradual, an erosion of sleep time as more things need to be done. As Dr. Richard Wyatt of the National Institute of Mental Health says, "If you are very busy, you tend to sacrifice sleep and learn that you don't need as much of it."[27] That's exactly what has happened in Dr. Dean Foster's life. Dr. Foster, a psychology professor at Virginia Military Institute who does research in the sleep field, says when he was young he slept seven to eight hours, but over the years—he is now in his sixties—"I just kept whittling back until it's now about five hours. I wish it were less. There are so many things to do on this planet, I want to get in as many licks as I can before I desert it. Life is just too exciting for sleep."

Motivation is again the key, and sometimes that motivation comes suddenly and prompts a deliberate decision to shorten sleep time abruptly, though most of us would be miserable without a period of gradual adjustment. For some an imposed new discipline can work. For example, when Roy Rowan, a senior editor at *Fortune,* was stricken with cancer five years ago— and he has made a remarkable recovery—he decided life is too precious to be wasted in sleeping. A lifelong eight-hour sleeper, he cut back to six and says he "feels fantastic." Similarly, an assistant professor at a university in New York City knew that the only way to forward his career was to publish. But he could never seem to get to writing during the day and at night he was too tired. So four years ago he started getting up at 5:30 A.M. instead of 7:30 A.M. (his usual bedtime is midnight) in order to get in two hours of writing while fresh. He went on to publish two books, and his third is in the works. (His story echoes that of the late Douglas Southall Freeman, who edited the Richmond [Virginia] *News Leader* for thirty-four years and who rose at four every day to write. He managed to turn out seventeen volumes, including a seven-volume biography of Washington and a four-volume biography of Robert E. Lee that won the Pulitzer Prize.)

Rowan and the professor took two hours off their accustomed sleep time, and that's the most that the majority of us will manage. But some people have achieved extraordinary reductions in their sleep needs. Gary Null, who writes and lectures on nutrition and health, says that fifteen years ago he "needed" eight to nine hours of sleep. Applying his principles of nutrition, exercise—he now runs ten to twelve miles a day— and meditation, he gradually cut back until he says he now sleeps only two to four hours a night, usually two, from 2:00 A.M. to 4:00 A.M. But his experience is rare and few of us are ready for the many disciplines he's introduced into his life.

For most of us, gaining one or two hours will prove a reasonable, realistic and welcome goal when we're trying to break long-established sleep habits. And we'll look at some sleep reduction experiments, carried out by university professors, that validate such an expectation. These experiments will in turn suggest the program that will eventually be spelled out in Chapter 7— a gradual, sensible, safe way of reducing one's sleep. For those who would like to try for an even greater reduction in sleep time, the program offers guidelines that will help you explore your own capacity.

But before we get into the program, we want to be absolutely certain that we won't be jeopardizing our physical or mental health to any degree when we eliminate accustomed sleep from our lives. And we'll begin dealing with that concern by finding out first what we know about sleep and what it does for us.

CHAPTER 2

Deep, Restful Sleep:
You Won't Lose a Minute of It

What exactly happens during sleep? After all, we should know what goes on while we sleep before we commit ourselves to a program that aims at curtailing that process.

Twenty-five years ago people knew very little about sleep. Scientists then called it a "unitary state of passive recuperation." You are awake, you drift off into a state of sleep and you stay there until you come out of it, as though—and primitive people believed this—the soul took flight to an unknown limbo for eight hours and then returned to the body. A scientific paper published in 1939 defined sound sleep as sleep without dreams.[1] Today, with our increasingly sophisticated monitoring systems, we know that all of us dream —and more than once—every sleeping night of our lives.

But this ignorance of the past is understandable. It's not easy, in fact, to find out what's happening to people while they're sound asleep. There were some crude early investigations—such as attaching wires to bedsprings to record how often people shift position in a night—and most of us, surprisingly, change position anywhere from twenty to sixty times a night.

What made possible real progress in the study of sleep was the development of sensitive instruments that measure various bodily functions while people are sleeping. Some of these instruments have been around since the 1930s, but their serious application to sleep research didn't really begin until the 1950s, led by Dr. Nathaniel Kleitman at the University of Chicago. Since then the work has expanded enormously every year. There are now sleep laboratories throughout the world, a 300-member Association for the Psychophysiological Study of Sleep and something like a thousand papers a year published on the various aspects of sleep. Though there is still a great deal we don't know about sleep, we've certainly learned more in these past twenty-five years than was known by mankind in all of its previous history.

One of the things we know is that there is continuous electrical activity—through the night as well as during the day—in the billions of individual nerve cells that comprise the brain. An electroencephalograph is the instrument that records this electrical activity; its sensitive amplifiers magnify the extremely small voltages that the brain cells generate. While the electroencephalograph is the key to the discoveries that have been made, two other instruments have been added to the researcher's tool kit: an electro-oculograph, which traces eye movements, and an electromyograph, which gauges muscle activity.

In laboratories where sleep is studied, a person about to retire for the night is wired up like a Christmas tree. In a process similar to that involving an electrocardiogram, tiny metal-disk electrodes attached to wires are taped to the body—in this case, behind the ears, beside the eyes, on the forehead, under the chin and in other spots, according to the experiment. The multicolored wires are gathered in a ponytail at the back of the head and plugged into a junction box; cables then lead to a recording polygraph machine in another room. The electrical impulses being gathered move a pen across an unwinding roll of paper. And something like 1,000 feet of paper are covered with the up-and-down squiggles during an eight-hour night. It seems all those wires don't inhibit sleep; people get used to them.

What the squiggles reveal is something you probably have read about already, for sleep labs have earned considerable attention in the press. Few of us aren't aware by now that sleep is a pattern of alternating cycles rather than one single state. But one thing to note first: the patterns of electrical activity generated during sleep are quite different from those that appear when we are awake. They even differ from those of people under hypnosis. When professors talk, say, about crocodiles being asleep even if their eyes are open, they mean that the patterns recorded on the roll of paper look different from those traced by wide-awake crocodiles.

The Sleep Process: A Series of Stages

To briefly review the sleep process: we get into bed, our muscles relax, our minds drift, then, *snap*, we're asleep. The onset of sleep is not gradual; it just happens, in a second. Says Dr. William Dement, "Awareness stops abruptly, as if ten billion furiously communicating brain cells were suddenly placed on 'standby' status."[2] We're in Stage One of sleep. The lines on the paper are huddled close together in a steady progression; from far enough away they look like a straight line. This is very light sleep, a threshold state; if we're awakened, we're hardly aware that we've been asleep. But the process is under way: gradually our temperature will be falling, our respiration and heartbeat slowing, our muscles relaxing, the amount of sugar carried in the blood increasing.

After about fifteen minutes we move into Stage Two. The lines on the paper become somewhat farther apart and bounce up and down more, showing short bursts of brain activity. If we're awakened now, it takes a few seconds to come out of it and we know we've been asleep.

When we reach Stages Three and Four, about a half hour after falling asleep, there is a distinct difference in what is being traced on the paper. The line is no longer crabbed; it spreads out into definite waves with a slower frequency and a higher amplitude. The waves our brains are making are called Delta Waves, and science writer Maggie Scarf says they "look like brain waves of deep slumber *ought* to look—lazy and easy and wide."[3] We are indeed in deep sleep, and there is no better definition of deep sleep than that it is the hardest stage from which to arouse anyone. The sleeper is remote from the "real" world and, if awakened, will require some seconds to become reoriented. A child awakened from Stage Four often takes minutes to return to full awareness. During Stage Four sleep-walking may occur, by the way, and those who talk in their sleep converse. Respiration and heartbeat are very slow.

And then, after about a half hour of deep sleep and an hour after sleep began, a reversal starts. We back away into Stage Three again, then Stage Two and then —something entirely different happens, so different that many sleep experts feel there are two basic kinds of sleep: the kind described up to this point, and that which follows. What follows, in fact, is so much more like a waking state than a sleeping one—the heart and respiration rates and blood pressure increase, for example—that it is often called paradoxical sleep. The muscles of the trunk, arms and legs go limp, as though paralyzed, but there is often visible twitching in the face and hands.

Watch your dog when he sleeps and you'll see all this happen. When he drops off, his respiration is slow and regular and he lies still and quiet. Then, in ten to twenty minutes, you'll see his breathing turn irreg-ular—rapid, shallow breaths followed by periods when he seems to be holding his breath. And his ears and whiskers will twitch and perhaps his face and paws as well. He may whimper, tremble slightly, grimace. You can watch it in a cat, too; at this stage of sleep, the cat's head falls, the muscles collapse—but again, the face and whiskers quiver.

REM Sleep: A Special Stage

During this stage, the pen moving across the unwinding paper traces a pattern very much like Stage One sleep, though more irregular. More blood is flowing toward the brain, and its temperature is up. Under closed eyelids the eyes are darting back and forth, a phenomenon first discovered in 1952 by Eugene Aserinsky, a young graduate student working with Dr. Kleitman in Chicago. Actually, if people close their lids and move their eyes, the movement is observable without the help of electrical instruments. But no one had bothered to note it before, and the medical world was astounded. "It would be difficult today," says Dr. Dement, "to understand how skeptical we were. These eye movements, which had all the attributes of waking eye movements, had absolutely no business appearing in sleep." Their discovery, he added, changed sleep studies "from a relatively pedestrian inquiry into an intensely exciting endeavor."[4]

During this stage the eyes dart back and forth, not regularly but intermittently, in bursts, as though the sleeper were watching a Ping-Pong game. We are sleeping, of course, but in this sleeping state the brain is active, telling the eyes what to do. The scientists say that it's also telling the body what to do, and that if nature had not contrived it so that the trunk, arms and legs were limp at this point, we would leap out of bed and be off, no doubt to do ourselves harm. It is a keyed-up stage of sleep. It's during this time, for example, that more gastric acid is secreted in ulcer patients, and it's when angina attacks often occur— some forty percent of all heart attacks happen during sleep (which has led some doctors to recommend the suppression of this stage, through drugs, in ulcer and angina cases). When the inhibiting mechanism in cats that makes physical responses impossible is surgically removed, they leap around their cages hissing and spitting.

This, then, is the portion of our nightly adventure called Rapid Eye Movement sleep or REM sleep. All the other hours of the night are often designated as non-REM sleep. It is during REM sleep that our dreams are much more vivid and easily recalled than during the rest of the night. And they tend to be more like what we think of as "dreams"—involving the unexpected, the imaginative, the emotional, the far-out. Non-REM dreams are more logical, prosaic, more like what happens in the waking state. (All our dreams, by the way, are in color, and researchers have found that some fifty percent of our dreams are about misfortunes and about a third are touched with fear and anxiety. Very few are about good fortune.)[5]

There's another curious feature of the REM state, and one that nobody can really explain: the increase of blood flow to the genitals. Males—babies and old men as well—have erections. In females, of course, the result is not as obvious, but temperature readings and photographs of the vaginal area show comparable stimulation. That doesn't mean that all dreams are erotic. Researchers have awakened people in the REM state (when awakened during REM sleep, an individual can recall the nature of a dream about eighty percent of the time) and asked them what they've been dreaming: overt sexual behavior is an uncommon occurrence in dreams—about one percent according to one study, eight percent in another.[6] And it is mostly of the milder sort—kissing and minor forms of lovemaking. Intercourse is very rare. When people do have sexual dreams, it's interesting to note that women usually dream of men they know, while men usually dream of assignations with strangers.[7]

The phenomenon of REM-period erections has led to an interesting therapy for men who complain of impotence. They are asked to spend a night in a sleep clinic. If they have normal erections during REM periods, there is nothing physically wrong. No erection, or a weak one (the degree is measured by "strain gauges" attached to the shaft and tip of the penis), indicates a physical dysfunction, and further tests are needed.

To digress yet another moment, what of blind people? Do they dream? This point was considered by Ian Oswald. He found that three subjects recently blinded continued to have normal REM periods of sleep. Three other subjects who had been blind since childhood also had REM periods, but there was no eye movement and they did not picture things. Their REM dreams were similar to the non-REM dreams of sighted people.[8]

But to continue on our nightly sojourn. It takes from seventy to one hundred and ten minutes from the time we fall asleep to go through Stages One, Two, Three, Four, Three, Two, REM—a total cycle. The average is ninety minutes. Ninety-minute cycles are quite common in our lives, though we are not aware of them. There are more than a hundred bodily functions—like hormone secretions and stomach contractions—operating on a ninety-minute cycle. Dr. Kleitman suggests that ninety-minute "rest-activity" cycles explain why we take a coffee break at 10:30 A.M.—ninety minutes after we arrive for work, ninety minutes before we go to lunch.[9] People who say they are fortified by ten-minute catnaps are probably grabbing for rest at the low end of a ninety-minute cycle. One study found that people isolated in a room with food, drink and cigarettes tended to put one or the other in their mouths every one hundred minutes, just off the ninety-minute cycle.[10] And another study that asked isolated subjects to keep a running record of their thoughts uncovered ninety-minute "fantasy cycles": at the peak of the cycle the subjects tended to fantasize, became emotional, had bizarre thoughts; then they swung back to the low end of the cycle and their minds reverted to their surroundings, concrete problems, the real world.[11] It's not certain that the ninety-minute sleep cycle is related to these others, but the whole phenomenon is curious and intriguing.

The first REM stage lasts five to fifteen minutes. Then the cycle is repeated, except that we move from REM sleep directly to Stage Two. If we sleep seven and a half hours, we'll go through five complete ninety-minute cycles, which means five dream periods. Since we can have more than one dream per dream period, someone has calculated that we experience some 150,000 dreams in a seventy-year lifetime.

About half the first three hours of an eight-hour night is spent in Stages Three and Four—deep, restful sleep. The REM periods are short. But they start to lengthen, and the last three hours of the night, the final two ninety-minute cycles, are quite different: Stage Three and Four sleep disappear and REM sleep takes over. The last REM period, just before we awaken, may last as long as an hour. (Contrary to what a great many of us may think, dream time and real time are almost always synchronous; that is, if in your dream you are being chased by someone for what seems like ten minutes, it is indeed ten minutes.) Through an eight-hour night you'll spend about fifty percent of your time in Stage Two sleep; about twenty percent in deep Delta Wave sleep, almost all during the first half of the night; and about twenty-five percent in REM sleep, mostly during the second-half period. Only about five percent is passed in Stage One.

And that's it. Far from being a "unitary state of passive recuperation," our nightly sleep is a series of states of very different qualities, one of them far from passive. Now that we've reviewed the sleep process, it's time to consider what we've learned, for it's extremely important to our concerns about sleep reduction.

The Deepest Sleep of the Night

We said that Stages Three and Four provide the deepest sleep of the night, because they are the time when it's hardest to awaken a sleeper. It would therefore seem that Stages Three and Four are those which give us the most rest, restore the tired body, and help us to awaken physically refreshed. We've also discovered that if we get no sleep for a day or two, our Stage Four sleep will increase on the subsequent night, which is evidence that we need Stage Four for recovery. There is also some indication that Stage Four increases after physical exertion, which further suggests its recuperative contribution.

Since there is much that we still do not know about sleep, however, we can't be certain about what Delta Wave sleep does for us. There are some puzzling aspects about this stage of sleep.

For one thing, as we get older, Stages Three and Four begin to disappear. In men, the decrease often starts as they pass the age of forty. At fifty, a third of all men no longer have any Stage Four sleep. Women resist this age change; a sixty-year-old woman shows the sleep cycle pattern of a man of fifty. But after sixty men and women spend more and more of their non-REM sleep time in the lighter Stages One and Two, which means they awaken much more often; Stages Three and Four usually eventually disappear altogether. So it would seem that we can't claim deep sleep as essential for restoration and survival.

Secondly, people sleeping in laboratories have been awakened every time they entered Stage Four sleep. It gets increasingly difficult to arouse them as the nights go by, but men and women have been deprived of Stage Four sleep for as long as seven days without any discernible consequences.[12]

Still, for most of our lives, Delta Wave sleep is something we need, or else we wouldn't demand more of it after being deprived of it. And it is the deepest sleep experience of the night. So it must be important to the sleep process as a whole. In any event, whatever special function it provides for our bodies needn't concern us, since a *sleep reduction program will not take away any Stage Four sleep*. Stage Four sleep, you see, is always bunched at the beginning of the night. *If we sleep four hours instead of eight we will still get just as much deep sleep*. This has been proved in experiment after experiment. If deep sleep does indeed restore our bodies and reverse tiredness, we needn't worry about cutting back, because we'll get just as much of it. Indeed, if we drop from eight hours of sleep to six, we are likely to *increase* our deep-sleep time.[13] Short sleepers are often called "efficient" sleepers because they pack in their deep sleep and then get out of bed.

That's why athletes can be short sleepers. People commonly believe athletes sleep longer, that they need more sleep to repair the strain and punishment they have taken during the day. But it just isn't always so. Many sleep fewer hours and get all the deep sleep they need to restore bodies put through much more tiring activity than the rest of us experience. Johnny Dziegiel, for example, the head trainer of the New York Giants, told me he knows exactly how many hours of sleep his men get—about six hours a night during the football season. During training it may be six and a half, but some players always average less than six. Off-season some players may sleep longer, but Dziegiel doubts it. And he says the men never complain about a lack of sleep. Hours of intense exercise don't evoke a need for more sleep. On the contrary, says Dziegiel, "because they are in great condition, they can practice and play from day to day with not much sleep."

Some athletes get by with amazingly little sleep. Consider Lenny Wilkens, who played basketball with the Seattle SuperSonics and is now their coach. The most he sleeps is four hours a night. "Even two hours of sleep allows me to function," he told me. And he never takes naps. He has slept only two to four hours all his life, "as long as I can remember." He reads or watches TV to 3:00 or 4:00 A.M. and is up at 6:00, feeling "great and ready to get going." He usually works out by practicing with the team in the morning and is convinced the physically fit person needs less sleep. He's never checked on his team's sleep schedules, as Dziegiel has, but he knows they need to unwind after a game and don't get to bed until well past midnight and then often have to be up at 6:00 A.M. to get an 8:00 A.M. flight to another city. So six hours of sleep is common.

Professional athletes are not the only ones to affirm the truth that physical activity can mean less need for sleep, not more. Studies have shown that exercise helps people sleep more soundly, and sound sleep is always more effective than restless sleep. And people who are physically active—who are full of energy and always on the move—are just the kind of people who curtail sleep so they can get more accomplished.

If we retain all our deep sleep when we sleep fewer hours, what kind of sleep *do* we lose? A lot of Stage Two sleep. Not much study has been done on Stage Two because if people are awakened every time they enter this stage—before they even get to Stage Three and Four and REM sleep—they are deprived of *all* sleep. What we also lose if we sleep less is REM sleep, because most of our REM sleep, remember, occurs in the last hours of the night.

A sleep reduction program therefore in no way threatens to lessen the amount of the deepest, soundest sleep of the night. Unless we start to sleep only two or three hours, we'll get exactly the same amount of it. It's REM sleep that is the swing factor in any sleep reduction effort. And less REM sleep means less dream time. Might cutting back on dream time hurt our minds, even if the retention of deep Delta Wave sleep has rested our bodies? REM loss is our next consideration.

CHAPTER 3
Dreams: Do We Need Them?

Dreams and their significance have both enthralled and mystified us throughout history. Since ancient times they've been viewed from countless perspectives: as sources of divination, as cures or commands, as journeys of the soul, wellsprings of art or reflections of our inner selves. Middle Eastern cultures of antiquity used dreams primarily to predict the future or as health remedies, stocking their literature with dream prophecies and opening their temples for dream rites to heal the sick. Iroquois Indians of the 1700s saw their dreams as official orders from on high, and any vision which appeared in a dream had then to be carried out in waking life. Nowadays, Eskimos of the Hudson Bay region believe that, as a miniature vacation from daily affairs, the soul leaves the body during sleep to restore itself in the dreamworld—while in Borneo, where dream is taken to be identical with reality, any man who dreams his wife is an adulterer will send her scurrying home alone to her father. And then there's the prevailing psychoanalytic view which considers dreams to be mirrors of the unconscious. Freud saw them more specifically as expressions of impulses, usually sexual in nature, that we repress when awake.

Fascinating as dreams may be, however, we won't look further at their significance except so far as our special concerns are involved. To the point: every night, all over the world, mankind sleeps. And when we sleep, we dream. And when we dream, something happens the purpose of which we don't fully understand. We *do* know that if we sleep fewer hours we will lose some dream time. Will we also lose something else? Do dreams serve some necessary psychological purpose? Are they essential to mental health? Will cutting back on dream time wreak emotional havoc?

Most REM dreaming, we've learned, occurs during the last hours of sleep, the very hours we want to curtail. Even most of us who are skeptical about psychoanalysis believe that dreams must serve *some* purpose, and we suspect that purpose must have something to do with handling our psychological problems. After all, who is making up our dreams but a part of ourselves? Won't we be in trouble if we take a portion of our dream life away?

We know for certain that even when we're asleep we continue to be aware of the events and problems of the daytime. How else can we explain the fact that a child watches *The Wizard of Oz* on television and that night has nightmares about wicked witches? Adults, too, have been shown distressing movies just before they went to sleep, and they did indeed dream about the material they had seen. People who have spent an evening in group therapy and then spent the night in the psychologist's sleep lab have dreamt about the problems stirred up during the session.[1] Psychiatrist Samuel Dunkell, in his book *Sleep Positions: The Night Language of the Body,* points out that couples who are no longer getting along will stay far away from each other in bed even after they are asleep and, if things get really bad, will actually kick each other during the night.[2]

It's interesting, as an aside, that studies conducted at the Veterans Hospital in Cincinnati by Drs. Milton Kramer and Thomas Roth revealed that our mood in the morning is related to what we have been dreaming —pleasant dreams can make us happy, frustrating dreams can make us belligerent.[3] The more people there are in a dream, by the way, the happier we are, regardless of the situation in the dream. Apparently mankind is gregarious by nature.

What Happens When We're Deprived of Dreams?

As it turns out, there's something else to consider: we seem to need REM time—whether or not for the sake of the dreams that occur then. First of all, if we try to deprive people of REM time by waking them whenever the EEG shows they are entering that stage of sleep, it becomes increasingly difficult to do so. They eventually just fall back asleep, skip all preliminary stages and go immediately into a REM period. We seem to have a stubborn need for REM sleep. Secondly, if we are deprived of REM time for several days, we have what is called a REM "rebound"—somehow we get reimbursed for some of the lost dream time and there is more of it on subsequent nights. The same is true, you remember, of Stage Four sleep, the other kind we seem to "need." The night after people have been deprived of all sleep for a long time, they get more Stage Four sleep; the next night they catch up on lost REM sleep. It's never a complete catch-up situation; that is, because you lost four hours of REM sleep you will not necessarily have four extra hours on a subsequent night—but the rebound is definitely there.

The first experiments conducted in REM and dream deprivation, moreover, seemed to confirm the fact that we need dreams to handle the day's psychological stresses. Dr. Dement, who conducted these early experiments, published his findings in 1960 and they made quite a stir.[4] It was then he made the discovery that it is increasingly difficult to suppress REM sleep and that REM rebound takes place on subsequent nights. He also claimed that depriving his subjects of REM sleep caused anxiety, irritability and difficulty in concentrating. He speculated that we need to discharge emotional trauma in REM dreams or we might suffer delusions, hallucinations and psychotic symptoms during the day. REM dreaming seems to be "in some way a necessary and vital part of our existence. . . ." It looked for a time as if Freud was right.

Dr. Dement's findings were so exciting that they spawned a rash of similar experiments. At first his conclusions were upheld. A Dr. Sampson reported similar psychological problems in people deprived of their REM time.[5] In another experiment Dr. Dement himself found that one subject deprived of REM sleep for sixteen nights displayed definite paranoid behavior and that another, who was normally staid and proper, expressed the desire after fifteen consecutive nights without REM sleep to go to a tavern, cheat the waitress out of drinks and then be off to a burlesque show.[6]

But the studies continued in a number of sleep labs, and soon the results began to look very different. There was no doubt about the persistent need for REM time, but the presumed psychological consequences of REM deprivation just weren't there: no evidence of anxiety, irritability, bizarre behavior and all the rest of it. People did not crack up when their dreams were taken away. The conclusion: either Dr. Dement's subjects were already very unstable types or the experience of the experiment itself—being awakened continuously night after night—had triggered strange emotional responses. Dr. Dement himself, looking at all the later experiments, admitted that he had been wrong: "a decade of research has failed to prove that substantial psychological ill effects result from prolonged selective REM sleep deprivation. We have deprived human subjects of REM sleep for sixteen days, and cats for seventy consecutive days, without producing signs of serious psychological disruption."[7]

Remember, these people were deprived of *all* REM

sleep—and there were still no discernible ill effects to the psyche. Dr. David Foulkes, author of *The Psychology of Sleep,* concluded, "Contrary to the Freudian position that the dream is an essential safety valve for the release of emotional tensions, it has become evident that REM-sleep deprivation is not psychologically disruptive."[8] That point has to be stressed because Dr. Dement's original report received so much publicity that many people still think REM loss is an invitation to mental breakdown.

Further Evidence That We May Not Need Dreams

If you still have any doubts about what the loss of some REM sleep might do to you, consider the following:

First of all, all animals whose sleep patterns have been studied on EEG machines show REM periods. If *they* are dreaming, do their dreams serve as the same subtle psychological escape valves? It seems absurd. The opossum, for example, which naturalists consider such a primitive animal that they have dubbed it a "living fossil," has as much REM time as man. Or listen to this wry comment from Dr. Ray Meddis, sleep researcher at the University of Technology at Loughborough in England:

"At the time of writing I know that the list of animals which show clear signs of the REM sleep state includes chimpanzee, baboon, macaque, rhesus monkey, goat, pig, cow, horse, sheep, rabbit, elephant, cat, bottle-nose dolphin, pilot-whale, seal, bat, guinea pig, rat, chipmunk, mouse, squirrel, hamster, mole, mole-rat, treeshrew, desert-hedgehog, armadillo, opossum, kangaroo, phalanger, owl, burrowing owl, domestic chicken, pigeon, hawk and falcon. With a list like this it is

tempting to wonder what they are all dreaming about."[9]
How would Freud answer that question?

But if REM sleep in animals casts doubt on REM
sleep's role in psychological stability, man as a species
presents a phenomenon even more difficult to explain.
We have noted that adults who sleep eight hours a
night spend about twenty-five percent of their sleeping
time in REM sleep. Newborn babies, however, spend
about half their sleeping time in a REM state, premature infants about seventy-five percent, and it is
thought that in intrauterine life sleep is one hundred
percent REM sleep. (The sleep of newborn kittens and
puppies is all REM sleep, EEGs show.)[10] If we wonder
what animals are dreaming about, what in the world
could be going on in the brains of babies? Certainly
it's reasonable to say that if REM sleep does serve a
function, that function may have nothing to do with a
dream response to the external world. How can REM
sleep, for example, be an outlet for suppressed desires?
What has the newborn infant suppressed?

And there's more to contemplate. If REM dreaming
serves a special psychic function, we should be able to
find some correlation between REM experience and
personality. But there doesn't seem to be any. Broad
testing shows that everyone, no matter what the personality type, spends about the same amount of time
in REM sleep. There is no increase in REM sleep time
during the psychologically difficult years of adolescence;
that is, there is no indication of increased REM
response to psychic need. Looking for some clue that
neurotics have more or less REM sleep than the well
adjusted, researchers have found none. Even the severely mentally ill—chronic schizophrenics, for example—
show no difference in their REM patterns.[11]

What is more, there is good evidence that instead of
helping people cope with psychological problems, REM
time may actually be a hindrance. It has been discovered that drugs given to depressed people to make

them feel better also happen to suppress REM sleep. And drugs whose side effect is to cause depression also increase REM sleep.[12] This has been a distinct surprise to researchers; in fact, all this evidence has been startling, for they, too, thought dreams must have something to do with helping people cope with the stress of life. But there have been many clinical cases reported that describe patients, given antidepressant drugs, who as a result have gone without any REM sleep for months and yet show a marked improvement in their ability to cope with stress and problems.[13]

In fact, some psychiatrists are treating depressed patients by asking them to sleep in a lab and then awakening them when they start their REM periods. Dr. Gerald Vogel conducted a three-year study on fifty-two mental patients at Georgia Mental Health Institute and found dream deprivation highly successful as a technique for curing depression. For example, a forty-nine-year-old woman who attempted suicide went through a three-week REM deprivation program and recovered enough to be sent home.[14] And a team of psychiatrists in Basel, Switzerland, report that sleep deprivation therapy "can be considered an astonishingly effective and simple method in the treatment of depression."[15] Says Dr. Meddis, "Not only does dream deprivation not lead to madness, it may even be useful as a cure for it in certain cases."[16]

So there appears to be no correlation between psychological need and REM time and no indication that we need REM sleep to maintain our sanity. In fact, if people are deprived of all REM sleep, as far as we can tell, nothing at all happens to them. But suppose there is something that REM sleep accomplishes that we don't know about: after all, we *do* seem to need it or else we wouldn't have REM rebound after we're deprived of it. Maybe we require REM time and our dreams for reasons we can't yet fathom.

You'll Still Retain Most of Your Dream Time

All right, but there are two points here. First, remember that even if you had no REM time you would still have dreams. We do dream in non-REM time, too —not as vividly, but just as certainly. As previously pointed out, a person awakened from REM sleep will remember what he or she was dreaming about eighty-five percent of the time. According to some studies, a person awakened from non-REM sleep will recall dreams fifty to sixty percent of the time—even seventy-five percent, in one study.[17] If we do need dreams, we aren't going to lose them totally even if we were to cut out REM time altogether.

In any event, no one's suggesting you sleep so few hours that you'll lose almost all REM time. Even though total REM deprivation may be harmless, you're not going to be anywhere near that state. And that's true despite the fact that REM time normally falls toward the end of the night, in the hours you intend to eliminate. For the brain soon makes an adjustment to your new sleep schedule *and REM time moves forward in your sleep hours at the expense of Stage Two.* If you've been sleeping eight hours and you start to sleep six, you will not lose all the REM time of that last two hours: some of it is captured by the six hours you do sleep. In fact, you'll retain seventy-five to eighty percent of the REM time you would have had with eight hours of sleep.[18] And losing those minutes of REM time is apparently meaningless. As Dr. Vogel says, even if REM loss could be presumed to be harmful in some way we don't know about, "minimal REM sleep protects against development of the presumed harm." Dr. Vogel concludes that REM loss simply "is not a cause or contributor to clinical illness in man."[19]

What has our look at the sleep process taught us?

First, as discussed in the previous chapter, that if deep sleep is essential to restore your body and maintain your physical health, you needn't worry, because if you sleep even four hours you'll get just as much deep sleep as if you slept twice as long. And while you will lose *some* REM dream time by curtailing your sleep, you won't lose much, and you really don't even need a fraction of what you will get to maintain your psychological health.

CHAPTER 4

A Search for the Purpose of Sleep

All right, maybe we needn't worry about Stage Four sleep and REM sleep, but how about the fifty percent of the night we spend in Stage Two sleep? Or what of the totality of the night's sleep—all the stages as a package, so to speak? Sleep is a necessity, so there must be some value to the process as a whole. Won't we suffer if we shorten or distort that process? One way to put our minds to rest about any ill effects from sleep loss is to consider what would happen to us if we were deprived of *all* sleep.

Obviously, we can't go completely without sleep for very long—eventually we would just collapse into bed and nothing could wake us. The longest most of us have gone without sleep is for one night, and a few of us have given up sleep for two nights. Usually, to our own surprise, we can function the next day: we're "out of it," a bit woozy, maybe incapable of doing anything really tough—but we do better than we would have guessed. At least we don't collapse. We have reserves, apparently, that can carry us through; when there's the pressure of something we have to do, we can still push some inner buttons for the additional energy needed to get it done.

But suppose we extend that one- or two-day stretch to several? Let's look at an extreme and see how bad the damage would be if we were to eliminate sleep totally for several days running. Experiments in sleep deprivation have been going on for almost one hundred years now. The first, in 1894, was on puppies in Italy; the researcher reported that the puppies deprived of sleep died within four to six days. To this day, you will see statements that "we"—people, that is—will die without sleep. In 1927 Dr. Nathaniel Kleitman checked out that early experiment. He deprived a dozen puppies of sleep for two to seven days. Death? Hardly. He noted no changes in heart rate, respiration, blood sugar, body temperature or white cell count.[1] And in all subsequent animal studies, as noted by Dr. Wilse Webb, who has published dozens of research articles on many aspects of sleep, there are "few clearly documented and consistent changes that could be ascribed to sleep loss."[2] Why that 1894 report, then? No one knows. None of these experiments are easy to interpret, even today. Suppose you deprive animals or people of sleep, then note that they become increasingly aggressive. Is it the absence of some internal process during sleep that makes them hostile, or the fact that some character in a white coat wakes them up every time they try to get forty winks?

The fact that the heart rate, blood count and other body functions aren't affected by sleep loss doesn't mean the animals don't get sleepy. Desperately sleepy. Rats deprived of sleep by electrical shocks sent to the floor of their cages managed to climb the smooth steel walls of their cells and hook their teeth into the mesh covering and, thus suspended, fall asleep! Yet it's extremely interesting to note that tender treatment works better in these experiments. Rats shocked into wakefulness every time they started to fall asleep could no longer be kept awake after eighteen to thirty hours; other rats stimulated by walking, handling, feeding and gentle attention were alert, eating well and in fairly good shape after four days without sleep.[3] Perhaps it is not too farfetched to read a lesson into that lab experience that you can apply to your own sleep reduction program: that if you cut your sleep by two hours merely to gain more time for work you are likely to abandon your program after a few days, but if you reduce your sleep gradually and gently and mix pleasures into your gained time as a reward, you are much more likely to stick with your revised sleep pattern and succeed.

Deprived of All Sleep, We Stay Remarkably Whole

When it comes to sleep deprivation in humans, we are not unlike animals: our bodies keep on functioning well but we get very, very sleepy—not just physical sleepiness, but the attendant inability to concentrate, the crabbiness, the low frustration level, the tendency toward depression. And while we may be able to get ourselves up for whatever it is we have to do after losing one night's sleep, when the job is done we collapse. If the pressure continues so that we *can't* collapse, we soon realize it's taking three times the effort that it normally does to get the simplest task done.

No, we need our sleep, all right. But what we want to resolve is the question of "how much?" Sleep experts attempting to answer that question have first tried to find out why we need sleep at all—what sleep does for us. So they've deprived some people (usually paid volunteers from some branch of the Armed Services) of all sleep for a prolonged period of time, say a week, to see what happens when sleep is taken away. The official record for sleeplessness is eleven days, although *The Guinness Book of World Records* claims that an Englishwoman, Mrs. Maureen Weston, went without sleep for almost nineteen days. This, then, is what can be reported:

General State. No surprises here: people deprived of sleep get increasingly, desperately sleepy. It gets harder and harder for them to stay awake. The groups of

volunteers have to keep after each other to prevent sur-
reptitious naps, and the research group has to be ever
more vigilant. The state of sleepiness is not unlike that
of drunkenness: speech becomes slurred and rambling,
filled with repetitions and mispronunciations; one walks
into things with eyes wide open; there is a tendency toward silly laughter; objects undulate and change their
size and shape. After three days, the volunteers no
longer have any will to read or keep their diaries or do
anything that requires the slightest concentration. The
urge to sleep is so strong that they start to doze for just
seconds with their eyes open—microsleeps, they are
called, detectable on electronic monitoring devices.

Performance. How well can sleep-starved people do
their work? In the laboratories they are given all sorts
of tests to establish and quantify performance levels.
How long does it take them to press a key when a light
goes on? How well can they group a batch of cards according to color, shape, design and border pattern?
How good are they at memorizing a number of short
items from an almanac? How adept are they at adding
a column of numbers?

For about three days a person's ability to keep going
isn't bad. The person may feel, subjectively, that it is
impossible to do what is asked, and the task may indeed
require much greater effort. But somehow, given the
assignment, that extra effort can still be made and the
test completed surprisingly well—again just as you
and I somehow manage to get a report on the boss's
desk after little sleep because he or she has demanded
it by 3:30.

In fact, experiments show that we can go three days
without sleep and still do our work reasonably well.
After three days, performance deteriorates rapidly for
about two more days; then a second wind seems to prevent any further sharp drop in abilities. It's a gradual
decline from there. But it's amazing how well we can
do without sleep. As an Office of Naval Research

manual stated, when advising officers about what will happen to their men under sleepless combat conditions, there are "no effects on the visual and auditory sense functions . . . body steadiness and reaction time are impaired but no other changes in motor control or performance have been noted . . . ability to do mental arithmetic, take an intelligence test, or do memory tasks is affected sometimes, but very frequently scores remain constant . . . complex performances show no clear-cut deterioration."[4]

What's fascinating is that even under the extraordinary strain of days of sleeplessness, interesting tasks can still be performed well, while monotonous jobs—the kind that tend to put us to sleep on the best of days—become overwhelmingly difficult and usually end in work that's a mess. Performance picks up as soon as a person is given something challenging to do. The French army conducted a study early in this decade, for example, that concluded even three days of sleep loss doesn't severely impair a soldier's fighting ability. Faced by the enemy, he'll do all right. Put in front of a radar screen, however, and told to sit there and watch it, he may manage to stay awake, but his mind will drift away so often that you can't depend on him.[5] It's the same old conclusion: if you have something to stay awake for, something that isn't tedious and dull, giving up sleep is far less of a problem.

Psychological Effects. Here you get wide variations, as might be expected, since people differ in their psychological stability. Two individuals who undertook a private war against Morpheus offer good examples of this broad range of experience. In 1959, Peter Tripp, a New York disk jockey, decided to go without sleep as part of a fund-raising drive for the March of Dimes and, no doubt, to gain some press coverage for himself. He broadcast from a glass-walled Army recruiting station at Times Square and lived across the street, in the late Hotel Astor. A gaggle of psychologists, psychiatrists and doctors monitored Tripp's progress. His health checked out without problems, and he was usually able to work himself up to a respectable degree of competence for his radio shows. But his mind was soon a mess. After two days without sleep, he was complaining that there were cobwebs in his shoes and that specks on the table-cloth were crawling bugs. After five days, signs of delirium appeared: a nurse was dripping saliva, a doctor's tweed suit was a field of furry worms. In another day he was screaming that his hotel room bureau drawer was filled with flames. He no longer knew who he was or where he was. Paranoia set in. On the eighth day he collapsed, literally fell into someone's arms. He then slept for thirteen hours and all the illusion and agony were over.[6]

Tripp was thirty-two. It was six years later, in 1965, that a seventeen-year-old named Randy Gardner set the official record of exactly eleven days. Young Randy had a much easier time of it than Tripp. He did suffer from blurred vision, slurred speech, memory deterioration (he even had trouble reciting the alphabet), a bit of nausea and pronounced irritability. But his motor ability held up remarkably well. On the last night of his vigil, Dr. Dement took Randy, who lived in San Diego, to an all-night penny arcade where the two of them played some hundred games of pinball-like baseball to pass the hours. Dr. Dement reports that Randy won every single game and that his mental state was largely untroubled. He had a few hallucinations, but nothing resembling the kind of psychotic behavior Tripp displayed. Randy must have been a much more stable person. After fourteen hours and forty minutes in bed, Randy was fit as a fiddle.[7]

Deprive a large enough group of people of sleep and you'll get the gamut of psychological responses. All will tend to become moody, morose and apathetic. And irritable—bickering and even heated outbursts are common. Some complain of a feeling of unreality, of separation from the self, and a confusion about who they really are. Minor hallucinations and delusions are also common—the sensation of cobwebs covering the face is a frequent complaint.

Probably the most striking reaction to sleeplessness to be recorded took place at UCLA's Neuropsychiatric Institute in the late 1960s. After seven days without sleep, one of four young adult men really went berserk. He screamed in terror, fell to the floor sobbing and begged to be dismissed from the experiment. He also muttered something incoherent about a gorilla. Psychiatric questioning revealed that at the age of five or six he had been frightened by a picture of a gorilla and had had nightmares about the ape—a terror that returned under sleep stress.[8]

But that sort of reaction is not usual. On the whole, truly "crazy" behavior is rare. A 1955 study of 350 servicemen found that by the third day without sleep seventy percent had audiovisual hallucinations, but only seven percent devolved into a state of acute psychosis.[9] As Dr. Webb has said, almost in awe, considering what the body is going through (the fatigue, rhythm changes and an overwhelming need for sleep), "the surprise lies in the relatively small number of unreal responses occurring. It is even more remarkable that these 'oddities' of behavior seldom appear before three days of deprivation and are seldom the most dominant behaviors even after five or six days without sleep."[10]

But, you may ask, what about the dire psychological effects of sleep deprivation when used in brainwashing, such as during the Korean War? What happened to those victims, and how can we explain the difference between the dramatically injurious results of their experiences and the relatively harmless experiences of the subjects just discussed?

Sleep deprivation is very definitely a part of most brainwashing techniques, though here it may be far more insidious than mere deprivation—waking the prisoner every fifteen minutes, for example, or allowing snatches of sleep at unpredictable times during the day and night to induce total disorientation. But sleep denial is only part of the combination of physical and psychological weapons involved. For starters, the prisoner is frequently kept in total isolation. With no one at all to talk to, he becomes emotionally dependent on the only human he sees—his interrogator. This isolation and dependency lead to a feeling of total helplessness, especially since his interrogator often threatens him with torture or death, or holds out the reward of better treatment if the prisoner cooperates.

Lack of sleep is almost always accompanied by a filthy cell, poor food delivered at irregular hours, shabby clothing, tobacco deprivation, humiliating bathroom regulations, the inability to bathe, identification by number instead of name, and by kicking, slapping and other forms of physical punishment. All these measures trigger a loss of identity and self-respect and increase the dependency, fear and disorientation of the prisoner.

This "softening up" process is accompanied by interrogations that sometimes stretch through a day and night, which can combine indifference, threats, sudden friendship and impassioned indoctrination. The disorienting humiliation and the skill of the interrogator result in a kind of nefarious behavior modification that brings confessions and conversions. Prolonged sleep deprivation, while effective in impairing judgment and heightening desperation, is only part of the total manipulation technique.[11]

Physical Effect. Whatever sleeplessness does to our ability to work and our mental state, going without sleep, even for a week, has surprisingly little effect on the body. The hands may tremble a little, the eyes may become difficult to focus and the lids may droop, and sensitivity to pain increases. But for five days there is no change in weight, heart rate, respiration, blood pressure or other functions and very limited change in the composition of blood and urine. After five days some changes do occur, but they are slight. As Dr. Ernest Hartmann states, "there are few clearly demonstrated chemical-physiological changes produced by sleep deprivation."[12]

So the conclusion we can draw from sleep deprivation studies is that if someone took *all* sleep away from you for a whole week, your health wouldn't be adversely affected, your ability to work would suffer but wouldn't disappear, and you might have some hallucinations but you aren't likely to develop the symptoms of a psychotic. The main consequence of sleep deprivation is to make you subjectively more and more sleepy—there's no denying that—but no other appreciable harm would be apparent.

Now no one's suggesting that you go without sleep for five days. Or three days. Or one day. But if you're looking for more time to do the things you've always wanted to do, you *can* take an hour or two off every night's sleep. Nonetheless, isn't it reassuring to know that were you to eliminate sleep altogether for a number of days running, it wouldn't be likely to cause any damage?

Why, Then, Do We Sleep?

At this point you must be thoroughly puzzled by a very basic question: if taking away sleep—deep sleep, REM sleep or all sleep—doesn't seem to harm us, then why do we need it at all? Perhaps, as someone once said, sleep is like sex. We may need it but there's no physical damage if we have to do without it. Then what *does* sleep do for us?

On the face of it, that sounds like a ridiculous question. We know what sleep does for us even if the professors—with all their sophisticated information from electrodes and EEG machines and polygraphs—

don't. We know we need it because we can't keep our eyes open past our usual bedtime. And that it accomplishes what we expect it to accomplish: it rests and restores us so we can get through the next day. When we've had "enough" sleep, we're no longer mentally sleepy or physically tired. And if we're sick it helps heal us. We know, too, that at times when we've been under a great deal of mental stress we tend to want more sleep and it seems to refresh us, clear the air, keep us going. And when we grow exhausted, sleep can become more important than life itself. If that sounds exaggerated, think of the soldier who falls asleep on night watch even in the face of probable enemy attack, or of the people who doze off while driving at sixty miles an hour.

Sleep's important, there's no doubt about it. But if we stop to think about it some more, we do come up with some interesting questions. If sleep is needed to restore a tired body, why do the longshoreman and the accountant sleep the same number of hours? Or the professional athlete and the bedridden invalid? Why do the elderly, who get tired so easily, often need *less* sleep than other people? If sleep restores a tired mind, why is it hard to fall asleep after a stimulating, mentally active day and easy to doze off after a dull and unchallenging one? Besides, we know that our brain cells are as active in a state of sleep as when we are awake.

The professors are not witless or idle, and—being human—they also get just as sleepy as we do. But they can't yet find answers to these biological riddles either. Despite the increasing wealth of data about sleep, they remain thoroughly baffled as to just how sleep makes us feel rested, what it does for either our brains or our bodies. Just *what* is diminished during the day that is restored during sleep? We once thought cells were regenerated during sleep; now we know that cell regeneration goes on twenty-four hours a day. If something is being restored through sleep, why do some animals sleep only two hours and others fourteen or more? Or why, for that matter, can some humans sleep only one or two hours and function just as well as others who sleep eight or ten?

The fact that so many of these basic questions haven't been answered makes it difficult for the professors to answer directly and clearly the central question we're asking at this point: how much sleep do we actually need? Listen to Dr. Demont of Stanford: "It would be pleasant to be able to give a brisk, authoritative reply, but we're unable to do that because our research has not yet answered the even more basic question, 'Do we really need to sleep at all?' Furthermore, a real beginning on this question is almost impossible because we do not know what it is that sleep accomplishes."[13] Or, as Dr. Allan Rechtschaffen of the University of Chicago says, "I feel better after sleeping, but why? I don't know, and nobody else does either."[14]

There is, in fact, a joke, told by Dr. Dement in one of his books, that the real reason we sleep is "to prevent us from wandering around in the dark and bumping into things."[15]

There is one professor, however, who has come out and said, All right, let's honestly face what our research tells us. Dr. Ray Meddis, the English researcher, thinks it is time "to rid the sleep concept of its centuries-old associations with the need for rest and recovery. In my opinion, there is no necessary connection between the two."[16] And Dr. Meddis doesn't stop there: "I am tempted to apologize for being preposterous [but my] theory is that sleep serves no important function in modern man and that, in principle at least, man is capable of living happily without it."[17]

Now there is a statement! We are edging toward cutting back on our sleep by twenty-five percent or so and here is an expert who comes along and says we could probably do without it altogether. He doesn't

know how to go about it—we would still get sleepy—
but it wouldn't do us any harm if we could. Sleep, in
other words, is just a colossal waste of time.

Other researchers aren't ready to go that far yet.
As Dr. Peter Hauri of Dartmouth says, "It seems ridiculous to say nothing restorative happens and it goes
against all common sense. And I, personally, don't believe it."[18] Yet he admits he hasn't a shred of evidence
to prove otherwise. Or, as Dr. Rechtschaffen puts it,
"If sleep does not serve an absolutely vital function,
then it is the biggest mistake the evolutionary process
ever made."[19] (Aristotle, by the way, long ago claimed
to know why we sleep: to allow us to digest our food.
Why else do we fall asleep after a heavy meal, and
why else do babies both eat and sleep so much?)

The Mysterious Chemistry of Sleep

If the men of science can't explain why we sleep,
that doesn't mean they don't have their theories. There
are two main camps. One school stresses the importance of whatever physiological processes sleep must
provide for us that we can't as yet identify. These
experts write about "hormone discharge," "accumu-
lation of metabolic waste products," "resynthesis of
brain tissue" and "changes in blood composition." Most
of this probing is tough going for a layman. Listen to
this one: "catecholaminergic systems could be restored
by some simple synaptic mechanism such as altering
membrane reuptake or catabolism of amines in the
synaptic cleft." Comprehensible or not, these theories
go only just so far, since those who propose them ad-
mit they are still tentative and purely hypothetical. We
just don't know that much about chemical changes
that occur in the body during sleep.

There *is*, however, one chemical change most of us
do know about. Progesterone is the hormone that is

made in great abundance by the bodies of pregnant women and that could explain the fact that women sleep so much during the first months of pregnancy. When progesterone is injected into the brains of cats, for example, they fall asleep. So that is at least one clue about the connection between body chemistry and sleep.

Another clue comes from the adrenal hormones given to treat depression: they seem to stimulate people to levels where they need very little sleep. Dr. Nathan Kline at Rockland State Hospital in New York State, who has done extensive pioneering work in treating psychological problems with drugs rather than verbal therapy, has found that the antidepressants he prescribes—he calls them "psychic energizers"—have had that effect on his patients. He tried one of these drugs, a monoaminoxidase or MAO inhibitor, on himself and found he was sleeping only three hours a night and feeling fine. But after two months, he stopped; he really couldn't know what the long-term effect of such a drug would be. Yet he wonders if one day perfectly normal people won't be taking a pill to reduce their sleep time to two or three hours a night.[20]

The theory is, then, that if drugs which create a chemical reaction in the body affect the need for sleep, the need for sleep must have something to do with chemicals in the body. When these chemicals are restored or depleted or whatever happens during sleep, we are left revitalized, motivated and optimistic. But as yet nobody knows what these chemical changes are, and to a skeptic like Dr. Meddis, they are theories that are only "little more than biochemical fantasy."[21]

If chemical processes that restore us *do* occur during the night, that still leaves unanswered the question of whether one set of processes occurs during REM sleep and another during non-REM sleep. What would seem to make sense is that deep sleep, Stages Three and Four, restores the body, while REM dreaming sleep does something for the mind. The professors have certainly tried hard to find out. They have noted, for example, that athletes in training, rats after sexual activity and babies after circumcision show increases in Stage Four sleep. Dr. Hartmann is the chief defender of the position that deep sleep restores the body and that REM sleep, in spite of what we reviewed in the last chapter, may very likely be a way of handling stress during waking hours.[22] There is also some evidence that REM sleep is helpful in the learning process; for example, subjects who did better in an intensive language course had increased REM sleep.[23] One theory postulates that in REM sleep the mind is functioning like a computer, processing all the information it has been fed during the day and storing what it needs to retain. In one interesting study, young adults wore inverted prism glasses so they saw everything upside down, and their REM time increased while they were adjusting to a topsy-turvy world.[24]

Dr. Laverne C. Johnson, of the Naval Health Research Center in San Diego, however, questions whether our sleep stages serve distinct functions. He deprived subjects of all sleep for two nights; then, during two recovery nights, let some sleep normally and deprived the others only of Stage Four or REM sleep. There was no difference in recovery patterns. Stage Four and REM sleep seem to offer no special recuperative powers. Sleep is sleep, and Johnson concluded that "the amount rather than the type of sleep appears to be the most important factor."[25]

Is Sleep an Anachronism?

There is another, second school of thought about why we sleep. And it is particularly relevant to our interest in the matter. This theory claims that sleep developed during the evolutionary process for survival reasons and is still powerfully operative even if its function is obscure today. It is now innate, an instinct, and even if it hasn't any restorative function, we need it because we're programmed in our genes to need it.

According to this theory, sleep was probably "invented" some two hundred million years ago when sea creatures crawled up on the shore. Land dwellers developed the habit of sleeping as a safety measure. During the day they had to be alert and ready to run away from danger. At night they couldn't be seen, but they could be heard, so the best thing to do was to stay still and quiet and out of the way. The rest would help them to run faster and farther the next day, and while they were resting they also ensured their inconspicuousness by staying asleep.

The behavioral adaptationists can point to good evidence in the animal kingdom to support this survival thesis. The elephant, for example, sleeps only two or three hours, because it needs all the time it can get to gather food for that enormous stomach. (When elephants are in zoos, with their meals supplied, they sleep a few hours longer.) But mostly it's a matter of predation: the predators that feel safe sleep long hours and those that are usually the victims of predation get by on as little as they can. Grazing animals (cows, sheep and deer, for example), often exposed in open fields, are very short sleepers. Squirrels, relying on the safety of burrows, sleep fourteen hours a day. The gorilla feels secure as well—man is his only real danger—so he, too, sleeps fourteen hours. The mighty lion sleeps sixteen. Truett Allison and Henry Van Twyver came up with other interesting examples: the Indian sloth bear, who is such a good fighter that even tigers steer clear of him, sleeps long hours; the African baboon, which sleeps in treetops growing in the scrubby savanna where foliage is thin, sleeps fitfully, fearful of leopards; the macaque monkey of Asia, by contrast, which sleeps in treetops where the foliage is dense and protective, sleeps long and well.[26]

And man? Man certainly once had much to fear from beasts, so he also decided to lie low while the sun was down. And the habit became his inheritance. But that fear hasn't been operative for centuries and centuries, and in recent history man has been able to illuminate his darkness artificially and make it like the day. Then isn't sleep an anachronism? Isn't it time to outgrow the need for sleep? It's just a useless throwback. We rub our eyes and yawn and think of bed when the clock points to eleven because of *instinct,* not because we are suddenly responding to accumulated fatigue. It's the old fear of a predator out there somewhere in the dark. Says Dr. Meddis, "If you think about it, the only people who normally see you sleeping are people whom you would trust with your life anyway."[27] Since, he continues, there is no direct evidence to support the belief that sleep has any direct association with restitutive processes of any kind, and since its adaptive function is no longer valid, "it is possible that the time spent in slumber is completely wasted."[28]

You won't find too many who will agree entirely with Dr. Meddis, Dr. Rechtschaffen, for example, says he just can't believe that sleep could "have remained virtually unchanged as a monstrously useless, maladaptive vestige throughout the whole of mammalian evolution."[29] But it's an intriguing thought. If sleep is only an adaptation to conditions that don't exist anymore, it really *is* nothing less than an anachronism. And if we can't cut out all sleep because the need has been built into us over the centuries, at least we can eliminate *some* of it. As Dr. Gordon G. Globus of the University of California at Irvine points out, we now know that most slow-wave deep sleep comes in the first few hours anyway and that REM deprivation seems to have no effect. Then, too, he says, "because of a number of factors such as less physical work to accomplish and better nutrition, our bodies may not need anywhere near as much sleep as we actually obtain, but our brains continue to impose this evolutionary anachronism on us." He surmises that sleep may well be "no longer adaptive" but an "evolutionary anachronism."[30] We therefore need to learn a new behavior to adapt to the world of today. Fewer hours of sleep are right in tune with the evolutionary process. It's the path we'll *all* be following one of these days, so why not be in the vanguard?

Dr. Mangalore Pai, a British sleep authority, is one who firmly believes that man's adaptation to the pace of modern urban life will lead to everyone's sleeping shorter hours. He says he has seen people in India living in primitive conditions who sleep nine, ten and even eleven hours a night; they simply have nothing better to do with their time. But when they go to the city, they immediately sleep far less because they are too excited by what they see and experience. The conclusion for Dr. Pai is evident: "It is part of man's evolutionary process that he should sleep less and less as he discovers more reasons for staying awake."

Those who are brought up in industrial societies, Dr. Pai continues, are bombarded with stimuli from earliest childhood. Television, movies and books excite the mind, submerging the desire for sleep. As the desire subsides, so does the need. With all the heightened mental activity of modern life, Dr. Pai concludes, "it is inevitable that physiological changes should follow. Reduction in hours of sleep is one of them. It's a sign of good health."[31]

CHAPTER 5

Sleep Efficiency: How to Sleep Better No Matter How Long You Sleep

---

Despite all the riddles surrounding sleep, there is at least one indisputable fact on which both research and common sense agree: the quality of our sleep is vital in defining and controlling quantity. And there's a corollary: quality makes quantity less important. We all remember nights when we had eight hours of sleep and woke up tired, and nights when we had six and felt just fine. As the late Dr. Morris Fishbein, once head of the American Medical Association, wrote, "Three hours of quiet, undisturbed sleep may be more refreshing than eight hours of tossing about while the mind fusses and frets."[1]

In other words, it's not only *how much* you sleep but *how well* that determines how you feel the following day. And long hours of fitful sleep, spent wrestling with bedclothes, are almost worthless when it comes to feeling refreshed and vigorous the next morning. As a matter of fact, a sleep reduction program in itself could well help the quality of your sleep. Short sleepers tend to sleep soundly while nine-hour sleepers are likely to toss and turn. As Dartmouth's Dr. Hauri says, "Curtailing time in bed seems to solidify sleep. Excessively long hours in bed seem related to fragmented and shallow sleep."[2]

Let's take a look, then, at sleep efficiency in general.

We can all profit from learning something about how to maximize restful sleep, however long we spend in bed and whether or not we choose to attempt the program of sleep reduction outlined in Chapter 7. And if you *do* intend to cut back on your hours of sleep, this chapter will be particularly helpful in getting you started.

But before we consider just what we can do to create the optimum conditions for a good night's sleep, a word of caution is in order: the suggestions which follow concerning the things you can do before going to bed won't have much positive effect if everything you've done up to that time of day denies healthy sleep. As Dr. Julius Segal of the National Institute of Mental Health has rightly said, "Good sleep is not the result of something you do immediately before retiring but of a style of life and a manner of daily living."[3] In a similar vein, Drs. Thomas Coates and Carl Thoresen of Stanford recently wrote, "Sleeping well depends on living well. Tense and hectic days make for turbulent and troubled nights."[4] If you smoke too much, eat too much or drink too much, your sleep will be affected. And if you're tense all day long, you can't expect a three-minute relaxation exercise and a glass of warm milk to send you off into sweet slumber.

Of course, it's often the mind and not the body that robs us of a satisfying night. Psychological testing, in fact, indicates that consistently poor sleepers tend to be troubled personalities. As a simple example, poor sleepers are three times as likely to answer "yes" to the question "Do you feel alone and sad at parties?"[5] And while we all go through periods when we have trouble sleeping because something is preying on our minds, what do you do if you are the kind of person who is incessantly troubled by one thing or another? In cases where weeks or months of worry corrode sleep, the only answer is to get professional psychological help.

That's not to say, by any means, that *all* sleep disturbances—ranging from chronic insomnia to narcolepsy (which afflicts its victims with daytime "sleep attacks")—spring just from the mind. As the increasingly intensive work in sleep labs points out, certain cases of sleep disturbance once thought to be psychological in origin may be physiological by nature and can be eased by carefully guided medical treatment.

We'll get back to sleep disturbances a little later in the chapter, but for now it should be noted that anyone experiencing major sleep disorders beyond mild insomnia does indeed need treatment and can't expect to benefit greatly from the following general advice. Nor should he or she undertake a sleep reduction program without consultation with medical authorities. There is, after all, little point in any of us attempting to cut back on our hours of sleep if we are suffering from sleep disorders originating in depression, for example, or in neurological irregularities.

But, assuming your mind and body are in relatively good shape and you're not abusing either to an appreciable degree, here are some helpful ways to smooth your way into efficient sleep.

The Best Remedy: Keep to a Regular Schedule

This is probably the single most important rule you can follow in establishing good sleep habits. And in some ways, it's one of the hardest. Whether for work or pleasure, we often have reasons to stay up later certain nights and then to compensate by sleeping later in the morning as soon as possible, most likely on the following weekend. Young unmarried people often have wildly fluctuating schedules, while those with families are frequently tied down to a more regular routine. Whatever your lifestyle, if you're interested in establishing sound sleep patterns, you should make every effort to go to bed and get up at the same time every day. If you habituate your body to a schedule, and regularly follow it, the schedule synchronizes your sleep with your body's natural rhythms—and the various metabolic processes that continue through the night. As Dr. Webb says, if you go to bed at 10:30 P.M. one night and 2:00 A.M. the next, "the sleep system is likely to be saying, 'What's going on up there? One night I'm supposed to be asleep at this time and the next night I'm supposed to be awake. Which is it tonight?' "[6] And the result is very likely to be disturbed sleep. One survey showed that the strongest predictive of "I go to sleep easily" is "I go to sleep at a regular hour."[7]

Two professors at the Santa Cruz branch of the University of California, John M. Taub and Ralph J. Berger, conducted several experiments to learn more about the effect of regularity on the quality of sleep. They had people sleep eight hours but vary their schedule from 8:00 to 4:00, 10:00 to 6:00, midnight to 8:00, and 4:00 to noon. In their professional language, "alternations in a customary sleep-wakefulness pattern may be more closely associated with the efficiency of human performance than total sleep duration . . ."[8] In plain language, *keeping fixed sleep hours can be more important to how you feel and how well you work than how much sleep you get.*

Hasn't it happened to you? You usually go to bed at 11:00 P.M. and get up at 7:00 A.M., but you're up at 5:00 one morning, and even if you then go to bed early that night, don't you end up feeling tired and out of it? That old saw about one hour of sleep before midnight being worth two after midnight simply doesn't hold; the important thing is regular hours, not which hours they are.

Of course, it's almost impossible to get to bed every night at the same hour, that's true. There's a child in your house who keeps you up two hours in the middle of the night with a nightmare or a toothache. You're anxious about a critical meeting in your office the next day and you sleep miserably. You're having a new affair and lovemaking lasts half the night, or it's an old affair and a quarrel is equally prolonged. But when one or another event keeps you up longer than usual, get up the next morning close to your regular time anyway. Undoubtedly, you'll be tired for a couple of hours, but chances are you'll snap out of it by midmorning. Then go to sleep a little earlier than normal that night. Remember, you don't have to make up every minute of lost sleep. As we've seen, people have gone without sleep for days, even a week, and then slept an extra five or six hours—even though they've "lost" fifty—and felt fine. If, for example, you get to bed two hours later than usual, don't think you have to sleep two hours longer the next night. One hour longer is plenty, and those who are vital and active will want no more than an extra half hour.

On weekends, too, don't lie in bed for hours later than your usual wake-up time. If you bedded down at your regular time, sleep a half hour longer at the most. After all, regularity is important for efficient sleep, and you can't attain it by ignoring the rule two mornings out of every seven. What's more, those extra weekend hours are a good time to devote to the chores and hobbies you can't seem to find the time for during the week.

Bedtime Rituals: Establish a Sleep Routine

Establishing a routine that is followed faithfully every night is simply an exercise in conditioning, not unlike sticking to regular sleep hours: the routine sets up a mental pattern that suggests sleep just as fixed sleeping hours "set" the body's metabolic clock. We all know it helps children to drop off to sleep if we sing them the same familiar lullaby when it's bedtime. Well, when it comes to sleep, adults aren't much different. An invariable routine repeated every night at bedtime will soon make our lids heavy. And if we can fall asleep quickly—instead of lying there tense and frustrated—we avoid launching into sleep in a way that's bound to lead to a restless night. Furthermore, conditioning works both ways: if your present sleep routine is not conducive to sleep, a change in routine can be a great boon.

First, consider all the little things you can do nightly, in the same order, in the same fashion, that eventually condition your mind to associate their initiation with sleep. Simple things like checking the windows and doors, the children and pets; turning down the heat; putting out clothes for tomorrow; washing up; saying your prayers—or, in the current mode, devoting a few minutes to meditation. The final snack or glass of sherry. Or maybe a hot bath, a particularly relaxing experience that too many of us—especially men—have sadly forgotten.

People develop all sorts of last-minute activities before bed and do them so conscientiously they can't get to sleep if they ignore them. Maybe your necessary act is emptying the dishwasher or shining your shoes. Dickens, when he traveled, had to check to be sure the head of his bed faced north, believing that otherwise he would miss the value of electric currents that flow from pole to pole. Barbara Walters has to write down a list of things to do the next day. Once on paper they no longer preoccupy her, and, like all such little steps, this routine leads her peacefully toward sleep.

There are some people for whom reading or TV is an excellent pre-sleep relaxant, and others for whom even the dullest material is too stimulating. Inevitably their minds start to work on whatever ideas the book or program suggests, and sleep is postponed by a flurry of thoughts. In fact, some experts in the field of insomnia are strongly opposed to any reading or TV-viewing whatsoever in bed. They claim that beds should be for sleeping and sex only, and that if you want to read or watch TV you should go into another room. In short: associate your bedroom with sleep and you reinforce your conditioning. But this must be left to the individual. If you find that such activities don't help you sleep but tend to keep you up longer instead, then do them before you go to bed and go to bed only when you are ready to sleep.

Then there's the question of another pre-sleep bedtime activity, sex. Sex is stimulating exercise for both mind and body, of that there's no doubt. But it's also relaxing. And many people say they can't fall asleep without sexual release. Well, maybe that's their particular form of sleep conditioning, but physiologically it's nonsense. Sex is a relaxant but it's not a sedative. Kinsey long ago pointed out that the feeling of relaxation after orgasm lasts only four to five minutes.[9] Besides, the partner who falls asleep immediately after sex is not likely to be appreciated by a bedmate who would like to exchange a few tender words after intimacy and may end up jostling the sleeping partner into consciousness. So it seems there's no one rule: sex may or may not a sound sleeper make.

In any case, whether it's sex, a book or no activity at all, the time comes to shut one's eyes. And here again, the final step of the nighttime routine can be a big help in keeping the mind clear of anxieties and anticipations until sleep arrives. What position you start out in doesn't matter, so long as it's comfortable for you and is the same every night as one more fixed element in the sleeptime pattern. Then, instead of letting your mind drift back over the day's events or ahead to tomorrow's calendar, find a method—and stick to it—that clears the mind and turns off that ever-calculating consciousness.

After all, that's why people count sheep. Or recall a particularly lovely landscape as an antidote to disquieting thoughts. One method which for many is unusually effective is to lie on your back, straight, your arms at your sides, and to concentrate intently on your breathing. Take a slow, deep breath, hold it for one second, then let it out gradually and repeat. It can also help to stare, with eyes shut, at the bridge of one's nose, or to focus on a white dot, triangle or circle or other simple shape or object you visualize in your imagination. The combination of focusing on a mandala while breathing rhythmically crowds out any other concern. And in a minute or two breathing gradually becomes less deliberate; it returns to normal as you drift into sleep. Sure, you could call it meditation, yoga, self-hypnosis or autosuggestion, but whatever you call it, it's been known to work.

Others find a simple relaxation exercise can do wonders. Here's how it goes. First tense one foot by pointing your toes away from your body. Hold that position for five seconds, then let go. Then point your toes toward your head, hold five seconds and let go. Do the same with the other foot. Then tense one leg for five seconds and slowly let it go limp. Then the other leg. (For the first few days spend just two or three seconds on these exercises to avoid getting a cramp.) Next tighten your buttocks, hold five seconds, let go. Then the stomach. Take a deep breath that tenses your chest muscles, hold it and then let it out slowly. Push your shoulder blades back, as if you were trying to make them touch; then forward in the same manner. Tense each arm in turn. Make a fist with your left hand, then your right. Squeeze your eyes tightly; clench your teeth and tense your jaw; raise your eyebrows toward the top of your head as high as you can. Finally, tense the entire body, hold five seconds and let it slowly melt away. When you tense up, do it hard, and when you relax, exaggerate the letting go, as though you were relaxing your muscles even beyond their normally relaxed state. If you're still jumpy, do it over again. The whole process takes only a couple of minutes and is a good way to head off tension any time of the day. You can do this while standing in an elevator or sitting at your desk, any place or any time. As we've seen, tension and stress during the day take their toll on quiet sleep that night.

A total bedtime routine—brushing your teeth and shining your shoes, reading, clearing your mind to ease it into unconsciousness—becomes a mechanism you can count on. It's a ritual that signals sleep to your brain. And if your present nightly preparations don't spell sleep—if instead they have meant frustration— change them. If you've been having sherry, try milk; if you've been watching TV, try reading or forget both; if you've found relaxation exercises don't work for you, learn to meditate. (More on this in the last chapter.) And when you've found a new ritual that looks as if it will work, stick with it. Constant repetition will condition you into associating that ritual with untroubled sleep, and help make going to sleep a simple automatic habit.

A Tired Body Seeks Rest: Exercise Regularly

We've all been told time and time again that a good day's exercise makes for a good night's sleep. But is it true? Does exercise improve sleep?

The answer is yes. That doesn't mean some longshoremen don't have insomnia and some bedridden people won't sleep like logs, but on the whole, as Dr. Hauri says, "A steady daily amount of exercise probably deepens sleep over the long run."[10] Common sense here proves reliable, and one of the first things many sleep experts tell patients having trouble falling asleep is, "Get some exercise. Being tired will help you to sleep."

You'll notice that Dr. Hauri said that steady, daily exercise is needed. When professional athletes are tested in sleep labs, they show a greater percentage of sleep time spent in Stages Three and Four, the deep sleep stages that may be the part of sleep particularly responsible for reducing bodily fatigue. An athlete who is injured and laid up for a time no longer shows that pattern. So if you play your sets of tennis only on Saturday mornings, it won't do much for your sleep. What you need is daily activity.

But that doesn't necessarily mean heavy exercise. You may jog daily for the sake of your cardiovascular system, and that's fine, but moderate exercise is all you need to improve sleep. A couple of miles of walking instead of driving everywhere, or regularly going up and down flights of stairs instead of riding the elevator, or even walking from your office to those of other colleagues you want to talk to instead of automatically picking up the phone—just keeping active instead of sedentary all day—can use up energy and help induce sleep. In fact, occasional heavy exercise is more likely to cause muscle aches and pains that keep you up rather than send you off. Most of us have gone to bed at times and found we were "too tired to sleep." What you want is just enough exercise to tone up your body, not put a strain on it. If you swim at the Y a couple of days a week, then try to walk a little more—a little farther, a little faster—the other five.

Obviously, you shouldn't exercise just before going to bed. Your dinner may have worn off, but don't stimulate your heart and lungs and raise your temperature just before trying to calm everything down for the night. A late-evening stroll is okay, of course (it's something Lincoln did before going to bed), but not calisthenics. What's not as obvious is that early morning exercise won't do much for sleep either; the effect of that exercise has worn off by late evening. Better in the morning than not at all, but the most beneficial exercise in promoting sounder sleep is undertaken in the afternoon or early evening, when you come home from work and just before supper.

Exercise consciousness is important for another reason, beyond its direct effect in tiring the body. We've just noted that how you spend your days is more important for sound sleep than anything you do a half hour before you turn in. And exercise is a fundamental part of any reformation in daytime habits, to get your body as well as your mind in shape for generally efficient sleep, as well as for the more active and productive life a sleep reduction program promises.

Guard Your Stomach: Don't Go to Bed Hungry, and Watch the Caffeine

These days when everyone seems to be on a diet—often a semistarvation diet, at that—advice about not going to bed hungry has particular relevance. It isn't just that you will wake up at 2:00 A.M. and raid the refrigerator, thus interrupting your sleep: there really *is* a connection between sufficient food in the stomach and the quality of sleep, and studies have shown that people who are losing weight very often complain of poor sleep.

No one is recommending that you give up your diet; just allow, in your planned caloric intake, for a *light* late snack—never ask your stomach to digest a large meal at bedtime—if you need it. That way you won't be hungry in the middle of the night and become restless as a result, waking up tired the next day.

What sort of snack? Well, as it happens, you can knock off two thirds with one nibble. You can eat or drink something that will not only stave off hunger but that actually may help you get to sleep more quickly. It has been demonstrated that an amino acid called L-tryptophan is converted by the body into serotonin, a brain chemical that induces sleep. While experiments are now under way to test L-tryptophan's effectiveness as a sleep inducer for insomniacs, at least one study of normal sleepers showed that an amount of L-tryptophan equivalent to that in a large meal (you can get this chemical in ordinary foods) can cut falling asleep time in half.[11] Foods high in protein are richest in L-tryptophan—milk, cheese, meats, poultry, eggs and seafood. So a *high-protein snack helps induce sleep*. You may want to munch on leftover meat or chicken, but chances are you had enough of that at dinner. Cheese on a cracker makes a nice choice, or Ovaltine or some beef broth. Or a glass of warm milk—which is, indeed, the sleep inducer Mother always said it was. (If you can permit yourself the calories, a milk shake with ice cream—also rich in protein—is another tempting and effective pre-sleep snack. But somehow, for many of us, a cold drink suggests a revitalizer rather than a sleep potion.) If you don't like the taste of milk but concede it helps put you to sleep, why not flavor it with cinnamon, vanilla, nutmeg, licorice or ginger?

You can also buy L-tryptophan in tablet form in health food stores (though it has not yet been approved by the Food and Drug Administration as a drug, it can be sold as a food supplement). Since it is a natural substance, doctors treating insomniacs see no harm in their trying it. Dartmouth's Dr. Hauri says some of his patients have been helped, but results are definitely mixed and inconclusive thus far.

So far as coffee, tea and cola drinks are concerned, avoid them. Yes, it's true—caffeine keeps people awake. It disturbs the sleep even of people who claim that it doesn't. It will affect some people more than others, of course, and a single cup of coffee after dinner may be relatively harmless for most. But a second cup should be avoided. Even during the daytime, excessive amounts of caffeine can disturb sleep that night. The same is true of cola drinks and tea, which also have caffeine. An exception is chamomile tea (made from an herb rather than tea leaves), which has actually been shown to promote sleep. Chamomile tea, however, is very much an acquired taste, and for those who never quite make the adjustment, a dollop of honey will help.

The False Promise: Don't Depend on Sleeping Pills or Alcohol

Sleeping pills—whether doctor-prescribed or sold over-the-counter—may be all right to tide someone over a few rough days, like the period after a death in the family (although tranquilizers would certainly be a better idea than barbiturates, since they're less harmful to the central nervous system). And there's no harm in a mild alcoholic drink—beer, a glass of red or white wine, sherry or port—in the late evening. But habitual reliance on pills or hard liquor to help bring on sleep is not only harmful to the body, it won't even help you sleep after a couple of weeks unless you keep increasing your intake.

Something like $100 million worth of sleep-inducing drugs are sold annually in this country by prescription. (Add to that all of the nonprescription drugs, tranquilizers, antidepressants and liquor consumed to help sleep and the figures are staggering.) It is estimated that about a third of all Americans over the age of eighteen believe they have had sleeping problems, that about 8.5 million Americans took prescription sleeping pills at least once in 1977, that about one quarter of those took the pills every night for two consecutive months or longer, and that two to three billion doses are swallowed annually.[12] Yet one quickly builds up a tolerance to these drugs, and the annals of doctors and sleep labs are filled with stories of patients whose addiction has led to massive dosages. The Stanford Sleep Disorders Clinic reported on one woman of fifty who had started on pills to help her sleep when the pain from a slipped disk was interfering with her sleep. Ten years later she was taking 2,400 milligrams of meprobamate, two grains of phenobarbital, 100 milligrams of desipramine and more than 2,000 milligrams of sodium amytal. Her insomnia kept getting worse anyway, so she added two to four ounces of bourbon to her nightcap. It took eighteen months to "dry her out," get her off the drugs and liquor.[13]

That's the first thing sleep clinics have to do in treating insomniacs who have become hooked on drugs —for sleep can improve only when they gradually get off the pills and opt instead for other cures. These drugs suppress REM sleep—and, to a lesser degree, Delta sleep as well—and therefore cause a lighter and more disturbed sleep. But the drug withdrawal has to be gradual, because if done abruptly those years of REM suppression are followed by a massive rebound causing terrible nightmares (which is why many people who try to stop taking barbiturates cold turkey are terrified into starting on them again). Alcohol has the same effect. And drugs and alcohol, in addition to causing poor sleep, can bring hangovers, dizziness, headaches and depression during the day.

Don't take stimulants to stay awake either. That, too, becomes a vicious circle—you need more and more pills to fight increased tiredness. The worst curse of all, of course, falls on those who must rely on one kind of pill to sleep and another to pep them up. Needless to say, this is a desperate hell that has nothing to do with our program, which promotes less hours of sleep without pep pills and sound sleep without sleeping pills. It's a natural process you yourself control so that you sleep less and better and feel fine the next day without any artificial aids.

The Best Bed: One That's Comfortable for You

As obvious as it may sound, a comfortable bed is surprisingly important for restful sleep. There are no set rules about hard or soft mattresses or waterbeds or type of boxspring or pillows or size of bed, since every variation has been tested with no demonstrable advantage to any one of the numerous places where we may choose to deposit our bodies for the night. If you have a back problem and need firm support, that's one thing, but for pure sleep purposes the choice is yours. Incidentally, the same is true of your position on that bed: it is simply not true that everybody sleeps better on their backs or on their sides, or straight or curled up like a cat. As you come out of REM periods, you'll keep changing your position all night anyway, even though you don't remember it in the morning.

But if you're *not* comfortable with the bed you have at present, or if you're *not* sleeping well and you think that might be the reason, make a switch. Try out different kinds of mattresses and see what's comfortable for you. The peace a change brings may be psychological only, but if it works, why deny yourself? People who can't sleep well get so conditioned against relaxing in their present beds that any change often helps dramatically. (Often they sleep better in the sleep lab, in a hotel room or on the couch in their own living room—wherever the conditioning doesn't operate.) And can you think of a better way to spend your money than on a new bed that helps you sleep better every night of your life?

What is true of your bed is equally true of your

total environment. Do whatever makes you comfortable, so that going to bed makes you feel good and relaxed and favorably disposed toward sleep. Don't underestimate the effects of the seemingly smallest things. If blue wallpaper is soothing to you—fine. If patterned sheets seem too "loud," avoid them; if, rather, you think they make the bed more attractive and inviting, then they're okay. Some people sleep best on fresh sheets, like Churchill, who liked a room with two beds so he could switch in the middle of the night and move into a clean one. Some can't sleep without a pillow, while others have found that removing their pillow has relaxed their neck muscles and made them more comfortable. What about wearing pajamas or sleeping in the nude? The same advice pertains: do what you prefer. And if you think a change might help, then make that change.

Keep Cool: A Warm Bedroom Can Hurt Your Sleep

Ben Franklin, you may recall, was a devout believer in the thesis that cold air promotes sleep. He slept with the windows open all through the winter and advised those who couldn't sleep to get out of bed and "undressed, walk about your chamber" to cool the skin. He himself was accustomed to sitting naked in front of a window in the morning reading a book, giving himself what he called his "tonic bath." A lot of people still think Franklin was right and that a cold bedroom is conducive to sound and healthy sleep. But there's no evidence to support that notion. If the room gets too cold, you'll probably wake up to look for another blanket. And the fact that your head remains exposed isn't going to help the quality of your sleep for the balance of the night.

However, there *is* evidence that when a bedroom is

too warm, it does disturb sleep. People wake up more, they toss around more, and deep sleep decreases. So while there is no ideal bedroom temperature, it shouldn't get much above 70 degrees—which is warm enough anyway and far exceeds the government's recent energy-conservation guidelines.

As for real summer heat, an air conditioner or a strong fan is a must. You can't sleep well lying in a pool of sweat. We all know people who complain that the noise of even the quietest air conditioner or fan disturbs their sleep, but with a certain amount of concerted effort, they can get used to it over time. In fact, tests show that a steady noise can even help promote sleep, especially if it drowns out other intermittent noises. In any event, a hot bedroom is no place to get a good night's sleep.

For Sounder Sleep: Keep Out Noises— and Light

While the steady hum of an air conditioner or fan may not disturb *your* sleep, sirens, rumbling trucks, planes taking off and other loud noises certainly will. Even if you think you are a person who can sleep through noise, since you've lived near an airport or busy highway for so many years that it no longer bothers you, you're wrong—noise does disturb the quality of your sleep even if it doesn't awaken you outright.

That's not to say that all people have the same tolerances when it comes to street traffic and other noises. Some people seem able to sleep through anything. Others seem especially sensitive to sounds. Older people, whose sleep is lighter anyway, are particularly vulnerable to noise, and women seem to be more sensitive to noise at night than men. It's also true that a mother may sleep through a thunderstorm but wake instantly when her child whimpers in the next room. What stage of sleep you are in when a police car screams by your house makes a difference, too; it's more likely to arouse you if you are in Stage Two sleep than in Stage Four—and if you're dreaming, the screech may be incorporated into your dream and never wake you up.

But whatever a person's individual tolerance, tests show that noises throw us out of our deep sleep or REM sleep into Stage One along with a likely shift in our positions. And Stage One, you remember, is a kind of light semisleep, when we are as much awake as asleep. While you'll wake up in the morning not remembering the noises that disturbed you and thinking you got a good night's sleep, you simply won't feel as rested because your sleep was actually disturbed.

We know this in large part from a study conducted early in the 1970s in Los Angeles that compared the sleep patterns of people living near International Airport with those living far from it. Even though those near the jets had lived there at least six years, they had, on an average, forty-five minutes less "useful" sleep (that is, Stages Two, Three and Four and REM sleep) than those who lived in quiet neighborhoods.[14]

So if you live somewhere where you can't avoid or muffle outside noises, try ear plugs. And if ear plugs bother you, then you are better off with some machine that makes a steady noise that masks the intermittent noises. That air conditioner, for example. Or a so-called white noise machine, available at select stores, which sends out a strong hum that should cover up most external noises; another machine will also provide the sound of rain or the surf.

What is true of noise is equally true of light: your bedroom should be dark, and if blinds, shades, curtains or drapes don't do the trick, wear eyeshades. Art Buchwald and Bess Myerson, two celebrities often on the lecture circuit, always pack eyeshades, just in case their hotel bedrooms have drapes that never quite meet in the center.

For Faster Drop-off: Wind Down at Night

What would seem an obvious imperative to anyone looking to drift quickly into trouble-free sleep is often violated: go to bed with as great a peace of mind as possible, relegating for another time of day any activities apt to trigger anxiety or excitement.

Even before you turn out the light in the living room and head for the bedroom, you should be tapering off the day's events in preparation for the hour of sleep. If, for example, you eat your dinner, relax for an hour or so and then pull out your briefcase and get involved with office problems or unpaid bills, they just may tire you out so that you can't keep your eyes open. But there's the larger likelihood they will get you keyed up. And even if you do fall asleep, you may wake up an hour later and have a hard time getting back to sleep because business or financial concerns come bubbling up to the surface. One sleep clinic treated a woman, a teacher of forty, who complained she'd had insomnia for twenty years. Her whole problem, the clinic discovered, was that she invariably procrastinated in preparing her lessons for the next day and kept putting them off until she was burning the midnight oil every night. Her sleep problem disappeared entirely when she got her work done earlier in the evening.

For that hour or so before bedtime, watch TV, read, play cards, talk or do something else quiet and relaxing, instead of doing chores and working right up to bedtime. Sure, it's hard sometimes, and impossible at others, but you'll certainly pay a price if you don't slow down most of your evenings.

Another point: perhaps you know some couples who have made it a rule to keep their conversations away from controversial subjects in the evening, and a very good practice it is. They scrupulously avoid all discussions of expenses, family visits or any other sensitive or sore points that are either going to start an argument or leave one party, or both, upset. We all tend to be touchier and less able to cope with problems late at night, so why not leave them to the next day or the weekend when they won't seem so monstrous or impinge on what should be the quiet time before sleep? Because we're prone to be cranky and irritable and contentious when we're tired, quarrels often arise late in the day. And they're no good for sleep—or for your sex life either, for that matter.

When You Can't Sleep: Get Out of Bed

Sleep is one aspect of life where trying harder doesn't help you succeed. All of us experience some nights when we lie in bed wide awake staring at the ceiling. We get up, we have a glass or two of warm milk, but it does no good. The worst thing you can do is lie there and fight for sleep, getting angrier every minute. Tension invariably mounts. If you can't just lie there and relax comfortably (which few people can do when sleep evades them), then get out of bed. Take up some quiet activity—a book, a hobby, a letter to a friend, an old movie on TV—until you feel sleepy again. You'll get back to sleep sooner that way and you'll save yourself a lot of frustration.

In fact, a psychologist named Richard Bootzin early in the decade developed a method of treating insomnia based on this very principle and, again, on conditioning.[15] If you haven't fallen asleep within ten minutes after turning off your light, get up and go out of the room and read or do something else until you feel sleepy. Then go back to bed. If in another ten minutes you still aren't asleep, repeat the process. Use your bedroom for sleeping—and sex—and nothing else, not reading, not TV. Get up at your usual time the next morning, despite how tired you are, and do not take any naps later that day.

The first night you may get no sleep at all. The next night, exhausted, you should fall asleep by two or three in the morning, no matter how severe your insomnia. And in two or three weeks you should be doing well, as you gradually become conditioned. More than half the people who have tried this program say it works: after four weeks they are falling asleep in fifteen minutes instead of in an hour or an hour and a half.

If You Still Have Trouble Sleeping: Get Help

There are some conditions that will disturb your sleep in ways no routine or exercises can overcome. Some of them are physical. As you get older, for example, you are likely to have aching joints and muscles that seem to make it impossible to get comfortable; a doctor may be able to prescribe medication that helps—and it could be nothing more sophisticated than aspirin. Another problem that bothers many people is a muscle condition called nocturnal myoclonus, which causes legs to twitch and jerk as often as every half minute or so at night, and for which a muscle relaxant may be the solution. Some people are troubled at night by something called sleep apnea, which can cause severe breathing difficulties that only throat surgery will correct. Diseases of the thyroid, kidney, heart and other organs can cause sleep difficulties, and sometimes medications taken for asthma, cardiac disturbances or other problems affect sleep patterns.

And then there's the sleeplessness for which there's no discernible physical cause; it's the mind that is our enemy. Sleep simply won't come, or it comes haltingly, in pale form, and we feel sleepy, tired, jittery and inefficient day after day. Surveys of doctors reveal that about fifteen percent of adult Americans complain of regular insomnia—and women suffer from it more than men. *Some experts estimate that as many as thirty million Americans have a real sleep problem.*[16]

Insomnia takes different forms. Some people complain that it takes too long to fall asleep—a half hour, an hour, more. Others report they wake up at four thirty in the morning and can't get back to sleep again. Still others say their sleep is too light; they keep waking up during the night and often lie awake for what seems an interminable time before dozing off again. And combinations of these afflictions are common, too.

Sometimes it helps to realize that the "sickness" one is suffering from is not that at all but a normal state. Old people, for example, sleep most of the night in Stages One and Two, which are lighter levels, so they do awaken more easily and more often. It can help an older person to make him or her understand that a pattern so different from that of greener years is not the result of an affliction or illness but of the normally changing patterns of later life. This may dispel at least some worry about sleeplessness.

Some people who wake up very early in the morning may actually be natural short sleepers who are trying to stay in bed longer because they think they must conform to a supposed norm. Every sleep clinic is consulted by people who have come in not because they feel tired during the day—they feel just fine on five hours of sleep—but because their spouse, a confirmed eight-hour sleeper, is convinced there is something wrong with anyone who sleeps only five hours, and harps on it so much that the short sleeper begins to wonder if he or she isn't an insomniac. If you sleep six hours or less but know you need no more to feel rested the next day, stop worrying. Get out of bed and stop trying to stretch out your sleep time. You are fine. In fact, you are lucky.

What is interesting about many who consider themselves insomniacs—that is, persons who swear they don't get enough sleep and feel terrible during the day as a result—is that a large proportion of them are not really insomniacs at all. Sleep clinics report that about *half* the people who come to consult them have no sleep problem in reality.

Consider: a group of sleepers at the clinic associated with the University of Chicago estimated it took them an average of fifty-nine minutes to fall asleep. Their actual average was fifteen minutes.[17] A sixty-one-year-old man came to a California clinic swearing he averaged four hours of sleep a night. In the four nights he spent at the clinic his true average proved to be eight hours and nine minutes![18] The Stanford Sleep Disorders Clinic treated a man who said his insomnia was so bad (he claimed he averaged less than five uneasy hours a night) that he couldn't work anymore and had to take an early retirement. Psychiatric treatment and handfuls of sleeping pill hadn't helped. He had become obsessed with his sleep "problem." In the clinic for two nights, however, he averaged seven hours and thirteen minutes of normal sleep. Staff members talked to the man, showing him his polygraph chart, and he was still enough in command of his senses to understand that he was all right, that his needless obsession was just that. He gave up his pills and his depression and later wrote the clinic that he had found a new lease on life.[19]

Since the clinics say that half the people who come to them are really sleeping well, one can't help concluding that a lot of people cling to the belief that they sleep poorly as an excuse to justify a lack of achievement or for other more complex psychological reasons. Let's hope this book, with its message that shorter sleep is a good and positive thing, will prompt at least some of those people to look again at their "insomnia" and ask themselves what is really going on in their lives. If they are getting "only" six hours of sleep, maybe they'll understand that that's all the sleep they need, and that if they stopped fixating on sleep they might discover what their true problem is. At least perhaps they will realize that it's anxiety and the struggle for more sleep that makes them tired the next day, not the fact that they are getting less than their ideal eight hours.

The British sleep expert Dr. Ray Meddis has tried to tell his insomnia patients just that, and he has also said as much to the press, although many people have hated him for it. One person wrote him a particularly angry note: "Somebody should catch hold of you. Tie you up and make you go a WEEK WITHOUT SLEEP. Then see how you feel. You are supposed to be a psychologist. In my opinion you are a Bloody Nut case. A menace to society."[20]

Dr. Meddis understands that there are millions of real insomniacs, whose sleep is troubled and shorter than they want it to be, and that they are miserable as a result. And even the pseudo-insomniacs are miserable enough, whatever the real reason, to seek professional help. And miserable people should be helped, and that is why sleep clinics have been set up in recent years. Sleep therapy is a very special field, and too many general practitioners and internists know too little about sleep and are too quick to prescribe sleeping pills to give a patient who's miserable some easy and quick relief, without considering what the long-term consequences can be.

The more we learn about sleep problems, the more we realize they are very complex and not prone to fast or universal solutions. But of some things we can be quite certain: *that you don't necessarily need eight hours of sleep to be rested. That if you're getting six or less but feel fine, you have nothing to worry about. That if you go to bed before you are sleepy and then worry because you can't fall asleep or if you worry instead because you wake up early feeling ready for the day—worrying because you believe you haven't spent the requisite hours in bed—you are worrying for naught.*

That occasional, even fairly frequent, insomnia is no cause for concern. That few people, no matter how well they have slept, wake up singing like larks. That just relaxing in bed can be restful, too, and can get you back to sleep faster than lying there cursing and struggling and fretting about how you will feel the next day, which intensifies your problem and poisons your life. That people can be tense even though they are sound asleep, to judge by the amount of tooth grinding that goes on at night, not to mention nightmares. That lack of sleep is very unlikely to hurt your health. That sleep per se is not necessarily the answer to all of life's problems. That sleep can't be blamed for everything that's wrong with you—that depression and irritability and fatigue may come from physical problems, like anemia or thyroid disorders, or from boredom, unhappiness over your job or a lousy love life.

That, in short, some insomniacs are not insomniacs at all, but people who have to be shown that they are sleeping as well as anyone and are using supposed lack of sleep to rationalize other problems. That some insomniacs could be converted to satisfied short sleepers with a change of attitude: a realization that six hours of sleep is enough, that if they sleep fewer than eight hours they should not be concerned but understand that six hours can be sufficient and efficient and refreshing and that they can use the extra hours to their advantage. That some insomniacs who are getting less than six hours of sleep, and troubled sleep at that, can be significantly helped by the simple routines suggested here, while others will need further help, whether psychological counseling, hypnotism, biofeedback or other forms of therapy. They need help and they should get it. A list of sleep clinics specializing in offering such help can be found in Appendix I of this book.

CHAPTER 6
Resetting Our Biological Clocks

We've looked into sleep researchers' laboratories and observed the men of science attempt to define the nature of sleep and what functions it serves; we've seen them deprive people of REM sleep and deep sleep and *all* sleep. We've considered how to make sleep, of however many hours, efficient and restful. Now, what about sleep reduction? What else do we need to know in order to convince ourselves it's worth a try? After all, we want to make certain that we aren't venturing into a program which is disruptive to the natural requirements and rhythms of our bodies. Have sleep reduction programs, in apparent defiance of those requirements, ever been carried out under controlled laboratory conditions?

Circadian Rhythms: They Don't Define Our Sleep Time

Most of us have read something about circadian (from the Latin *circa,* "around," and *dies,* "day") rhythms, the internal rhythms of almost all living things that are in tune with the twenty-four-hour cycle. Plants lower their leaves at night, fish stop swimming, clams rest quietly and all insects, reptiles, birds and mammals sleep. Some creatures, of course, are immobile during daylight—owls, bats, mice, spiders, skunks, cockroaches and more. The length of the sleep or rest period varies widely. Cows and sheep sleep only two or three hours daily, while cats sleep fourteen and the sloth, living up to its name, some twenty hours out of twenty-four. Looking at the inexorable pattern of nature's laws, many people wonder if one of them isn't mankind's need to sleep seven or eight hours during the diurnal cycle. After all, most people do, which is some evidence of its "naturalness." If we sleep eight hours, nature will reward us with a rested body and fresh spirit; if we don't, she will punish us for our disobedience.

It would certainly seem that nature requires us to spend part of every twenty-four-hour cycle in sleep, which is why no one credible has yet been discovered who does without it. And as we've seen, our bodies do go through phases with a twenty-four-hour regularity. Sugar levels drop and rise, for example, so that there's an optimum time to administer insulin to diabetics. Alcohol and even aspirin affect us differently at different hours. Some surgeons believe we are able to withstand the shock of surgery at some hours better than at others, and Dr. Franz Halberg of the University of Minnesota, a pioneer in this field, believes we should be able to find the time of day when chemotherapy or irradiation will be most effective.[1]

But that doesn't mean we are programmed for eight hours of sleep or any other specific number. What it does mean is that we have the opportunity to make our own sleep timetable regular and thereby gain nature's reinforcing assistance in achieving more satisfying sleep.

Just the fact that four-, five- and six-hour sleepers have checked out as sound as eight-hour sleepers should be enough to dispel any fear that nature demands eight hours of us. But beyond that, the circadian rhythms are not all that sacrosanct either, at least not with man. Man has more flexibility than a sloth. An example common to all of us is flying to a different time zone. We fly from New York to San Francisco. At 11:00 P.M. New York time we get sleepy but it's only dinnertime where we are now, so we have dinner when everyone else does and get to bed dead tired; then we wake up at our usual New York time of 7:30 A.M. and groan to see our travel alarm reads 4:30. But for the life of us, we can't fall asleep again. Our internal clocks are set to New York time.

Yet jet lag doesn't last forever. Those internal clocks get reset to match the ones on the wall. It'll take some people longer to adjust than it takes others, but in two to five days we usually start to feel comfortable. And in two or three weeks the body temperature curve makes an adjustment, along, eventually, with heart and respiratory rates, blood pressure and composition, hormone production and all the other functions that are part of our circadian rhythm. The body *can* adjust to change. *If you cut back your sleep time, the body's internal clocks will adjust to those changes as well.*

(It is interesting to note that some researchers, no doubt on a government grant, flew honeybees from the East Coast to California and found that, sure enough, bees suffer jet lag too; but they also learned to adjust after several days in the environs of Hollywood.)[2]

There's another obvious example of man's ability to alter his internal rhythms to changed circumstances: all those people who work on night shifts. The adjustment is not easy, but certainly many do it. If you start to sleep from 9:00 A.M. to 4:00 P.M. every day, and you do it day after day, your internal rhythms gradually conform to your new hours. As Professor Frank A. Brown, Jr., of Northwestern University puts it, "a clock-timed phenomenon within the organism may become uncoupled from the underlying clock."[3]

Of course, when men lived in caves, it made sense to be outdoors hunting while the sun was out and in one's cave, hiding from those animals and enemies, when it turned dark. Undoubtedly, that's when mankind's circadian rhythms were set. Candles and kerosene lamps made a big difference, but they were clumsy and expensive compared to electric lights. Edison himself said that sleep is a "heritage from cave man days. Now that we've got electric lights, we may be able to change all that."[4] If you subscribe to an evolutionary theory to explain the phenomenon of sleep, you can see why artificial light may one day mean all of us will be sleeping less.

Scientists have challenged the inexorability of circadian rhythms originally established by the cyclical light and warmth of the sun. Plants and laboratory animals have been brought into an environment where artificial means provide constant light and warmth. While circadian rhythms can be surprisingly persistent, changes finally start to happen, in varying degrees depending on the species. And, as it turns out, man has the highest degree of adaptability. Back in 1938, Dr. Nathaniel Kleitman took himself and an associate into Mammoth Cave in Kentucky. For a month they lived on a twenty-eight-hour day: nineteen hours with battery-operated lights and nine hours of darkness. Dr. Kleitman had a hard time adjusting, but in about one week his companion was getting sleepy when the time to turn off the lights approached and slept well for the subsequent nine hours.[5] And there have been several similar experiments since. In 1977, for example, a man in a study sponsored jointly by Harvard and Montefiore Hospital created a thirty-eight-hour day: he stayed awake twenty-two hours and slept sixteen.[6] One person even lived a ninety-minute "day"—an hour awake followed by a half hour of sleep. Dr. Kleitman has concluded that "it appears there is no foundation for assuming that some cosmic forces determine the twenty-four-hour rhythm. . . . On the contrary, the rhythm seems to be conditioned by the activity of the organism."[7]

Exactly. And if a twenty-four-hour rhythm is not

ineluctable, certainly the hours we sleep within it aren't either. Change your activities, your sleep schedule, and a new rhythm will soon be established. When you stick to a reduced sleep schedule with regularity, the pattern you have established will help you fall asleep and get up easily at the hours you have set. Nature will adjust your biological cycle to help you feel "right" with less sleep than you had before.

Experiments that have reset internal clocks to a new periodicity are certainly pertinent to our concern, but has there ever been a more direct attack on the problem? Again: have there ever been sleep reduction experiments conducted under controlled laboratory conditions? There have, and the results are very revealing indeed.

Cutting Back: Some Actual Experiments in Sleep Reduction

The first experiments—those before 1970—were crude, but they did tell us a few things that are important. The sleep time of subjects was reduced by a couple of hours for just one night up to a week, and the experiments confirmed what we have already learned: Stage Four sleep is very stable—that is, you can take away hours of sleep and not lose any deep sleep at all —and REM sleep "moves forward" in the night's cycles so that if you cut back from eight hours to six, you'll only lose about a quarter of your usual REM sleep.

Then, in 1974, Dr. Wilse Webb tried a more ambitious study. He put sixteen young men, normally seven-and-a-half-hour sleepers, on a schedule of five and a half hours for a period of sixty days. One man dropped out, but the other fifteen finished the program without incident. Dr. Webb reported that the reduction in sleep time had only two discernible effects: there was a slight decline in "auditory vigilance," measured by ability to respond to repetitive signals (which may have been nothing but the result of boredom with the endless testing), and it was hard for the subjects to get up in the morning. But by the eighth week, that had begun to disappear; drowsiness was at "normal levels" and they had no difficulty staying up until bedtime. Dr. Webb concluded that, at the least, someone who had to get by on less sleep for a while needn't be upset. He may fuss about getting fewer hours than he is accustomed to, but "at least our findings indicate that he may be assured about the sleep loss itself."[8]

A year later another report came out of a sleep lab in Ontario, Canada, written by Drs. Robert Ogilvie and Sidney Segalowitz. They reduced the sleep time of fifteen subjects—nine men and six women, aged eighteen to thirty-one—by approximately twenty percent, from eight hours to six and a half, for three weeks. Again everyone was fine. Some eyestrain was reported at first, but it disappeared by the third week. Performance measurements showed no impairment of ability to work. The fifteen were tired for a time, and irritable, but the doctors saw that disappearing, too: "Lengthening the study would have allowed some subjects to adapt more completely to the restricted sleep, for there are trends in the mood scale data which show most subjects' scores returning toward predeprivation baselines."[9]

Encouraging as these experiments were, they had one major flaw: they took people who had been sleeping seven or eight hours and cut back their sleep time abruptly. What was needed was a program of *gradual* sleep reduction.

In 1973, Dr. Laverne Johnson and Dr. William L. MacLeod, his colleague at the Naval Health Research Center in San Diego, reported on the results of just such an experimental path: they wanted to see, they said, "whether it would be possible for a person to shorten permanently his sleep time, by this gradual sleep reduction process."

Three San Diego State University students, one twenty-one-year-old woman and two men, nineteen and twenty-eight, were chosen. First they slept their customary seven and a half hours, while undergoing "baseline" tests. Then every two weeks they cut their sleep time by a half hour. They were doing fine until they reached the six-hour level; after that they began having trouble getting up in the morning and increasingly they complained of sleepiness. They needed more time to adjust, but they kept on going. When they reached the four-and-a-half-hour level, they were really having trouble staying awake and performance test results were deteriorating. One subject overslept a full three and a half hours; afternoon naps exceeding an hour happened more than once. The three became irritable and some signs of paranoia appeared. The nineteen-year-old dropped out. The remaining pair made it to the four-hour level and stayed there for three weeks. The experiment was over, five months after it began.

What is most interesting, however, is that Drs. Johnson and MacLeod contacted the two who had completed the marathon eight months later. How long were they sleeping now, on their own? The woman said she was sleeping six hours a night, a one-and-a-half-hour daily gain in awake time. The man reported he was now comfortable with five hours of sleep a night—a two-and-a-half-hour gain! (Later he told Dr. Johnson he was then sleeping five and a half to six hours, still an impressive gain.) Both said they had learned they could get along with less sleep and were delighted. Drs. Johnson and MacLeod concluded, "Our findings suggest that one can reduce his usual sleep time by use of a gradual sleep reduction schedule but, during the reduction period, changes in mood, performance, and sleep parameters may occur."[10]

The San Diego—Irvine Experiment

Dr. Johnson, intrigued by his findings with just two subjects, began to plan a more ambitious experiment. He worked this time with two colleagues at the San Diego Naval Health Center and three others from the University of California at Irvine, all with impeccable credentials. They published the results of their ambitious study in two articles in *Psychophysiology* in 1977.

For this experiment they selected a larger sample—four couples, all undergraduate or graduate students, aged twenty-one to twenty-eight. Six of the eight were normally eight-hour sleepers; one couple usually slept six and a half hours. Again, all would start at their usual levels and be tested at those levels, then start to reduce their sleep time by a half hour every two weeks. When all the subjects reached the six-and-a-half-hour level, however, they would have three weeks to adjust before attempting a further descent. If they managed to reach the five-hour stage, they would have a month to adapt before stepping down still further. The total experiment might take anywhere from four to six months, depending on what sleep level each subject attained. It was agreed that whenever anyone felt he or she just couldn't go on anymore, that person's participation would be over.

The subjects slept in their homes as usual and monitored themselves. They kept logs in which they recorded their total sleep time (TST)—night sleep plus naps—as well as how they were feeling and what they were experiencing during the day. They were to carry on their lives as usual. It was decided that all would go to bed later as the experiment progressed, but awake at the same hour.

Though the subjects themselves were the keepers of their sleep regimens and daily diaries, they were under continuous scrutiny. Electrical sleep recordings of each of the eight were taken, in their homes, three nights a week. There were periodic, thorough physical examinations at the San Diego Naval Health Research Center. They were subjected to batteries of tests with names like Stanford Sleepiness Scale, Feeling Tone Checklist, Williams Word Memory Test, Digit Span Test, Wilkinson Auditory Vigilance Tasks, Wilkinson Addition Test and one with the prepossessing name of the Minnesota Multiphasic Personality Inventory. A Profile of Mood States recorded degrees of tension, depression, anger, fatigue and what is called "bewilderment." The participants talked to psychiatrists regularly as well.

Two of the eight-hour sleepers reduced their sleep to five and a half hours before they gave up, two reached the five-hour level and two made it to four and a half hours. The couple that started at the six-and-a-half-hour level stopped at five hours.

To summarize the results of this extremely instructive and important experiment:

Health. The participants were very tired toward the end, but physical checkups revealed "no indications that the TST reductions . . . posed a threat to the health of . . . subjects."[11]

Performance. Measured by the tests, there was no reduction in ability to function as usual, and "no diminution in capabilities on the job or at school was reported."[12] The subjects themselves said they felt less efficient, "but this change did not appear on any of the objective tests."[13]

Psychological State. The group became so tired the last weeks that they tried to conserve their energy, and the researchers noted a "dampening of emotional involvement"—but one which they said was not equal to depression. In fact, "no major psychological changes were observed."[14] There was one piece of bizarre behavior: one unlikely subject—normally very staid in his social behavior—had a "streaking" episode during which he ran naked around his neighborhood. But aside from this one embarrassment, the scholarly team concluded that "as a group the subjects remained on an even keel."[15]

In other words, these eight people weren't hurt in body, psyche or ability to function even when they reduced their sleep as much as three and a half hours. But they did get sleepy. There is no point in softening the truth that changing one's long-held habits can be rough —for a while. It took a week to ten days at each level before the group began to feel comfortable. And it got rougher for them once they were below the six-hour level. They complained of fatigue a great deal then, in their sleep logs and to the psychologists and psychiatrists interviewing them. At the five-hour level, incidents of oversleeping became common, and the subjects couldn't seem to help snatching a nap in the afternoon. Said one, "I am noticeably less efficient, less energetic; for example, I can't seem to study as long as I used to. I get discouraged more easily, slightly depressed about overcoming difficulties, very much like I feel when I am sick with a cold."[16] But that was below the six-hour level. *Most eight-hour sleepers are just not going to be able to cut back to five hours—although some will—at least in the length of time these people were allowed to adjust.* As the researchers said, "there is a possible genetic level (except for a few persons) beyond which sleep cannot be reduced."[17] This is important to remember, and we will honor that limitation in our sleep reduction program.

(Two other interesting notes on the experiment: Three members of the group experienced hunger pangs at odd hours, but no one put on weight. And one couple reported that the extra hours awake "enriched their sex lives."[18] Below the six-hour level, however, some said they were too tired to make love.)

After a Year: One to Two and a Half Hours' Less Sleep

But that's not the end of the story. One year later the researchers went back to the eight subjects to check up on them. How many hours were they sleeping now? *Not one of the eight-hour sleepers had reverted to his or her old, established habits.* It was just like Dr. Johnson's earlier experiment. The two six-and-a-half-hour sleepers had gone back to that length, but the six eight-hour sleepers were sleeping *one to two and a half hours less* than they used to. And they felt perfectly comfortable—no fatigue—after casting away a good portion of their sleep. One of the eight now felt fine, had no trace of sleepiness, or any desire for more sleep, after five and a half hours of sleep a day; another, after six hours.

The research team's conclusions: *"gradual sleep reduction may be an effective way to reduce TST by one to two hours and may permanently alter sleep habits or requirements."*[19] Not just "habits" but "requirements." A new natural "need."

Yes, the word "may" is in there. That's the way professors have to hedge things. After all, just because all the tests came out negative doesn't mean there wasn't something wrong that they couldn't detect. And Dr. Johnson asked me to please express his "reservations" about sleep reduction for most people. "Why add another hour of frantic accomplishment when you can spend that hour in bed?" he asks. "My feeling is, if you have a comfortable cycle, don't fuss with it."

And he's right—if you prefer that hour in bed. This program isn't for everyone. It's for those who want to get out of bed and have that hour or two for more living.

It's true that the participants in the experiment were relatively young. But that makes no difference. Dr.

Johnson told me that he has met many middle-aged people who have cut back on sleep and find their new level "comfortable and enjoyable." It's also true that the adjustment process can be tough for some people, but Dr. Gordon Globus, an Irvine researcher on the project, told me he thought the eight subjects had done well because of the lock-step approach, with its chance to adapt to successively lower levels of sleep—and that's a process we can certainly emulate. Dr. Joyce Friedmann, another member of the Irvine group, told me that a number of the subjects informed her it would have been easier for them if they could have slept longer on weekends or gone at an even slower pace, something we'll keep in mind when we plan our own program. Dr. Friedmann happens to be a firm believer in the theory that our sleep needs are inherited, dictated by our genes. "But not totally so," she recognizes. "For some people, it looks like they can be comfortable with two or so less hours of sleep a night." Indeed they can.

The California study really says it all. Most people not suffering from major disturbances can cut back their sleep time by one to two hours. We can't, and shouldn't try to, push our sleep reduction program too far, but we have, as the report stated, "some plasticity with respect to sleep length . . . it can be adapted to conform to a changed life style."[20] We'll feel fine and be glad we made the effort. It won't be easy for a time, but any change in habits of long standing takes some struggle. And once we've added an hour or two to every single day, we'll know it was worth it.

CHAPTER 7

A Fourteen-Point Sleep Reduction Program

It's time now to step back and ask ourselves what we have learned and how we can use what we've learned to cut back on our sleep time with the least possible discomfort and the greatest possibility of success.

First, we have had it reaffirmed that we do indeed need sleep. But we've also seen that many people sleep only one or two hours, and that these short sleepers have been examined by physicians and declared fit and sound. There is no "norm" of seven or eight hours that we must all conform to in order to take care of our bodies and minds. "The range is fantastic," Dr. Laverne Johnson told me. "Just don't follow a fictitious norm, but establish your own comfort level." If you are already a natural short sleeper but you have been worrying about it, stop. You're fortunate.

We've very carefully explored what might happen to those of us who are not natural short sleepers when we cut down on our present sleep time. Very little, the doctors tell us, even when the reduction is radical. When researchers deprive people of sizable amounts of sleep—even of all sleep—they can't find any significantly harmful effects. They say that if we sleep four hours instead of eight we get the same amount of Stage Four or deep, restful sleep. They say further that if we reduce our sleep time we *will* lose REM dreaming sleep, but (1) if our cutback is modest we won't lose enough to cause concern, and (2) we're not sure we need any of it anyway.

We stopped to consider why we do indeed need sleep at all. One school of thought with impressive credentials and evidence in hand says it is probably a phenomenon of evolution, an adaptation to the early conditions of mankind. This suggests that it's time to adapt to the present century and get out of bed. All of mankind could very well be evolving toward fewer hours spent in unconsciousness.

We touched on the thesis that people who are disturbed or under stress want to sleep more. Furthermore, all researchers agree (and common sense dictates) that we have to be motivated to shorten our sleep hours, and a motivated person is one who is energetic, forward-looking and achievement-oriented. Someone who is in good shape emotionally and physically should therefore have an easier time cutting back on sleep. And someone who isn't may find that reduced sleep may not be possible until psychological and/or health problems are solved. In any event, we can all learn to make our sleep more efficient, and we investigated the steps we might take to improve its quality.

Finally, we looked at some experiments in sleep reduction and discovered that our biological clocks are not so fixed that we can't gradually adjust them in order to gain waking time. The conclusions we can draw from all these findings suggest the fourteen-point sleep reduction program that follows.

1. Define Exactly What You Want to Do with Your Gained Time

Don't start a sleep reduction program with some vague notion that "Sure, I could use an hour or two extra a day" or "There are a million things I could do with more time." Recognize that without strong and specific incentives, that pillow will be very hard to give up in the morning. *Motivation is vital, and it will be a big help if your motives are sharply defined. Know exactly what you intend to do with your new time.* That means on your first day of reducing your sleep you will be spending the extra time you gain in some way that you wouldn't have had time for otherwise. That way you build your enthusiasm for what your sleep reduction program is accomplishing and develop an appreciation of the growth in accomplishment as the program progresses. Your recognition of the change taking place will give you momentum as you proceed. Keep the carrot visible and it will help you over any hurdles.

2. Start Only When You Are Rested

It would be foolish to undertake this program at a time when you need, if anything, additional rest—when you are, or just have been, under unusual stress and/or experiencing what appear to be major sleep difficulties. Or when you've been sick and you know—or your doctor tells you—that you ought to wait awhile. Similarly, if you are heading into a difficult period, postpone the program. It wouldn't make sense to launch a sleep reduction program at the same time as you are about to have a new baby or begin a new job. You want to start from your regular level of sleep and concentrate—during a fairly normal period of activity—on a basic change in your pattern of life.

3. Begin with a Two-Week Base Period and Keep a Daily Sleep Log

You have to know where you are before you can figure out where and how far you're going. If you're reasonably certain that on most nights you're getting, say, eight hours of sleep, *start this program by sleeping two weeks at your regular level*—in this case, eight hours per night. And begin a daily log that records your total sleep time, including night hours *plus* any naps. That way you can double-check yourself and be assured you're harboring no delusions about how much sleep you've actually been getting.

But the main reason for this two-week "baseline" period is to make you aware, as you start this program, of just exactly how you feel with your usual amount of sleep. You may find that on some days an internal alarm goes off earlier than your bedside clock and that maybe you're "oversleeping" as far as real need goes. You may have a day or two when you're under great stress, or are just experiencing the "Blue Monday" syndrome, and recognize that you're sleepy even with eight hours and that "feeling good" is not necessarily tied to eight hours of sleep. You may discover that after a night when you sleep very soundly you seem to wake up earlier.

This point is that you need an orientation period before you begin reducing your sleep time, a period that establishes two important areas of self-awareness: a realization of how subtle the relationship can be between sleep and feeling states and a true sense of how you feel now, so you can compare that feeling to how you will feel later at lower sleep levels. When you're at the six-hour level and come home tired after a miserable day at the office, you'll realize you used to get just as worn out after such a day even when you were getting *eight* hours of sleep.

Many of us, however, don't know for sure just how much sleep we're getting now—because we go to bed later than we realize on an average or on an uneven schedule, or because we sleep later on weekends, or because we take naps we tend to forget about. *If you are not reasonably certain about your present sleep level because the pattern is so erratic, take one initial week to jot down your sleep hours in your new log.* If you've slept six and a half hours one night, seven hours one night, seven and half two nights, eight hours one night and nine and a half hours on Saturday and Sunday, you've averaged about eight hours. Then you can move into your baseline period for the next two weeks, trying to smooth out your schedule so that you get close to eight hours every night of the week. Regularity is important to this program, as we shall shortly stress.

Keeping a log throughout the program—recording not only how many hours you're sleeping day by day but how you're feeling as well—is not an option. It's absolutely essential. You need the discipline of putting down on paper exactly how many hours of sleep you get daily; otherwise you'll make vague estimates in your head and kid yourself about how you're doing. The log will give you perspective: setbacks for a few days won't look like disasters if you can view the progress you're making overall. And including short notes about how you're doing—"Very tired this afternoon" or "No trouble at all getting out of bed this morning"—is of considerable help. Beyond providing explicit information with which to monitor your progress, such notes also function as a kind of sympathetic and encouraging dialogue with yourself. Cutting back on sleep time is a lonely internal process, and there is a limit to how long your friends and relatives will want to listen to a running narrative of your daily mental and physical states. Put it all down in your log. (For a suggested model, see Appendix II.)

4. Be As Regular in Your Sleep Hours As You Possibly Can

We've seen the importance of sticking to a regular sleep schedule in maintaining sound sleep. It's equally important in promoting shorter sleep. And a regular schedule means two things: (1) *Stick to the same number of hours of sleep per night.* If you're at the seven-hour level, for instance, try to get seven hours—or as close to that as you can—every night rather than going along with an irregular schedule that averages out to seven hours; and (2) *Get those hours at the same time every day.* For example, on a seven-hour schedule, try to go to bed at midnight and get up at 7:00 A.M. every day rather than vary that routine with an 11:00 P.M. to 6:00 A.M. stretch one night and 1:00 A.M. to 8:00 A.M. the next. One study showed, you recall, that regularity of hours may be more important than number of hours of sleep in deciding how we feel the next day. When you establish a rhythm that puts your sleeping and waking hours in synch with your body's metabolic timer, you give yourself a big assist in carrying out sleep reduction goals.

The usual pattern in a sleep reduction program is to go to bed a half hour later as you enter a new phase and get up at the same time. But if you're a lark who likes the morning hours, go to bed at the same time and get up a half hour earlier. What matters is the regularity from day to day.

Of course, all of us have nights when our usual schedule has to be broken. But just do the best you can, and keep in mind that the more irregular your hours, the harder the adjustment will be. And don't try to average out every minute of sleep. That is, if you are at the seven-hour level and oversleep a half hour one day, forget it; don't cut back on your sleep the next night but get your usual seven hours. If you get an hour's *less* sleep, don't feel you have to get an additional hour the next night; get an extra half hour, if you're feeling tired, and then get back on your seven-hour schedule the following night. As we've seen from sleep deprivation studies, every minute of "lost" sleep doesn't have to be recaptured in order for us to feel fit again. What's more, be tolerant of yourself. If you need a little more sleep at times, bend the rules of the program so that it can succeed.

5. Reduce Your Sleep Time Gradually

This rule is absolutely crucial and should never be bent. If you've interpreted this book's message as "You don't need as much sleep as you've been getting, so start now to sleep two hours less," you've wholly misunderstood it. The sleep pattern you have developed over the years is a firmly established habit now, and if you suddenly alter it radically, you will simply be exhausted and fail. *The whole premise of this program is that a gradual reduction in sleep time gives the body and mind time to adjust to moderate changes, step by step.* As Dr. Globus, one of the professors who conducted the California experiment described in Chapter 6, told me, "Our subjects handled the reduction pretty well because, as it were, they sneaked up on it. They had a chance to adapt to a new regimen."

Reduce your sleep time in half-hour segments. If your two-week base period was spent at eight hours, the third week—the first when you're really starting to cut back—sleep seven and a half hours. Quarter-hour reductions, for most people, are too short to be practical, but half-hour differences are substantial enough to deal with.

Give your body, your mind, your internal clocks plenty of time to adjust to each new level. With an adjustment period long enough to bring familiar comfort at one level, starting at the next level becomes less traumatic. You have to work your way down, dig in and build a comfort base there before trying your next descent. That's something I learned by failing, at first, to do so in my own reduction effort. Although adjustment time will vary from person to person, to some extent it's a function of age. The young, with sleep habits less firmly established, are usually more flexible. I would suggest the following schedule:

Ages twenty to thirty: three weeks' adjustment at every new level until you reach six and a half hours. Then four weeks' adjustment at six and a half hours and any level below that.

Ages thirty to forty-five: four weeks' adjustment at every new level until you reach six and a half hours. At six and a half hours and lower, give yourself six weeks.

Ages forty-five to fifty-five: four weeks' adjustment to seven hours. Then six weeks' adjustment at six and a half and six hours. If you go below six hours, give yourself eight weeks to adjust at each lower level.

Over fifty-five: you're on your own. As many people get older, they feel less need for sleep, and I hope this book has helped you understand that this is normal and not at all harmful. But sleep often begins, too, to become lighter and more disturbed, and many older people feel the need for naps to supplement what they consider unsatisfying night sleep. These people are looking for increased restful sleep, not a reduction in sleep time. Perhaps following this book's suggestions for improving the quality of sleep, and trying to achieve a solid package, say six and a half hours, of good sleep rather than lying in bed eight or nine hours hoping to catch snatches of additional sleep, will be helpful.

Any older person who still has the zest to do more in life, and who feels it is better to learn later than not at all how to create more hours in the day, can certainly try this program. *Just give yourself plenty of time— even two or three months—to become accustomed to, and comfortable with, a new level of sleep.* But give it up if you're not adjusting well. It would be folly to push yourself too hard after a lifetime of one kind of sleep expectation.

6. Be Prepared for Discomfort Until You Adjust to a New Level of Sleep Time

Because your sleep habits are so entrenched, you've got to expect initial stress when breaking them. Until you get used to a new stage of your reduction program, you'll be sleepy, tired, less efficient—or *feel* less efficient, at any rate—perhaps cranky and hard to get along with, and you may feel some physical discomfort like burning eyes. You, and those around you, must be prepared to put up with these upsets, but they shouldn't last long—a week to ten days at each level can be expected. But exactly how long and how much discomfort will vary from person to person. For some, the transition will be fairly smooth; for others it may be discouragingly difficult. If it's too difficult, if after ten days to two weeks you're not adjusting well, give up that level and return to the last level at which you were comfortable. You can try again later.

If after three weeks of following this program, *any* reduction in your usual sleep time—even a half hour—leaves you feeling upset, so that you don't think you're adjusting at all, this program is probably not yet for you. You may be someone with a psychological need for more sleep, or your attitude about sleep needs may be too ingrained, or your motivation is just not strong enough. The vast majority of us who have been sleeping seven hours or more can adjust to a sleep reduction of at least one hour, but there may be some people who can't. And if they can't, they won't; sleep will simply overtake them.

7. Don't Push Too Hard

Be honest with yourself. If after ten days to two weeks you're not adjusting well, stop and go back to the previous level. You can try again in another month, and if the program still doesn't take, you've reached your limit. There's simply no point in pushing too hard. *Accept the fact that there is a limit—perhaps an inherited limit—to how much you can reduce your sleep.* I suggest the following targets:

If you now sleep this number of hours:	You should be able to reduce your sleep time easily to this level:	And you should finally be able to achieve a reduction to at least this level:
9 or more	8	7
8½	7½	6½
8	7	6
7½	6½	6
7	6½	6
6½	6	6

Don't go below the last number unless you feel very comfortable at that level. Six hours is postulated as a kind of reduction limit. Six hours—or five and a half—is a major accomplishment. "Short sleepers" are usually described as those who sleep six hours or less; there aren't many people who can get by on five or less. If you are now sleeping six hours or less a night, you are very likely already at your limit, or close to it.

At these lower levels, you are really in the realm of experiment. You are trying to see how far you can go and still feel okay. Some people will be able to do it; it is really a question of age, physical condition, motivation, personality adjustment, amount and type of exercise one is getting, the food one eats and a host of other factors. Some people will be testing, too, to discover whether or not they are really natural short sleepers who have been oversleeping in order to conform to supposed norms.

For those now sleeping more than eight hours, guidelines are difficult to establish. No experimentation has been done with long sleepers. It may be that just as five- and four-hour sleepers are at one end of the distribution curve, nine- and ten-hour sleepers are at the other, and that neither has a great deal of flexibility. If Dr. Hartmann is right, long sleepers need more sleep to obtain more REM time, and that need reflects a personality troubled by psychological stress. Should the ability to cope with the environment improve, it might be possible for long sleepers to reduce sleep time more than I've indicated.

There is another factor to consider with long sleepers, too: many have been shown in labs to be people who stay in bed for nine hours but sleep eight; they are simply poor sleepers. If their sleep remains inefficient, so that it takes a considerable time before they fall asleep and they then go through several awakenings during the night, these sleepers won't be able to cut back very much. But it's very possible that trying a shorter sleep period at night—and *sticking* to it even when sleepy and tired—will lead to sounder, more efficient sleep. They may find that they're as refreshed with six and a half hours as they once were after nine hours in bed. Here again, experimentation is necessary.

These targets are reasonable and conservative. They are based on actual experiments that have been carried out and on what we know about sleep and sleep habits. The major study in sleep reduction to date—the California experiment that reduced eight persons' sleep time—concluded that "adequately motivated persons following a gradual sleep-reduction regimen are likely to attain sleep durations one to two hours less than habitual eight-hour levels."[1] Aud Dr. Hartmann wrote that "it is definitely possible . . . for someone to train himself to change within a range of perhaps one hour around his usual requirement."[2] When I pressed Dr.

Hartmann, he added, "One hour—maybe two hours." I have been just as cautious in my suggestions.

But individuals are just that—individuals—and some of them will be able to go further. They will find, perhaps to their own surprise, that after a time they are very comfortable with the six-hour level and can work their way down to five and a half or five hours of sleep, perhaps even fewer.

8. Try Going One Step Beyond the Sleep Level You Hope To Obtain

The sleep reduction chart, accompanying point 7, gave what should be an easily reachable goal and a second goal that should be attainable with greater effort. But there are no absolutes, and to a large extent you're experimenting to see what lower sleep level is truly comfortable for you. The only way to find that level is by probing—to give a still lower level a try and see if it's a possibility.

While your program is experimental and the outcome unknown, you are nevertheless probably starting out with a specific anticipated goal in mind: "I'm sleeping eight hours a night now. It would be great if I could cut down about an hour and a half." In that case, if you do reach six and a half hours, give six a try for a week to ten days. Either you'll find that six hours is becoming comfortable, too, and you can therefore reduce your sleep time even more than you had hoped, or you'll see that six hours is not working and you'll revert to six and a half. If it doesn't turn out to be a successful downward step in the reduction process, consider it a kind of helpful "stretching" exercise. For there's a very good chance that six and a half hours will now seem even more comfortable than before.

So far as my own experience was concerned, six and a half hours of sleep was *not* a terribly successful routine the first time I tried it. But when I tried six anyway—and grew increasingly irritable, with dizzy spells and stomach discomfort—it was clear the jump down was premature. By comparison, my move back up to six and a half hours of sleep, on second go-round, established a level of thoroughly acceptable personal comfort. And about a month later I was able to try again for six hours, this time successfully. And it's interesting that those who reduced their sleep time in the California experiment also went beyond the point where they eventually settled in. There was no analysis of the psychological justification for sleep stretching, and we can't be certain it will work for everyone. But it's certainly worth a try.

And what do you do if you reach the six-hour level? The same rule applies: if you are very comfortable with six hours, you may want to see if you can't do even better. Or if six doesn't feel quite right, attempting five and a half may then make six seem very right indeed. But it doesn't continue forever, unless you're really going for broke—trying to see if you're a four-hour sleeper. At the lower levels you will sense that you have reached your limit, that you haven't the motivation or confidence in your physical and mental state to attempt another drop. I myself felt that way about six hours and just stopped. You know yourself well enough to recognize when further probing will be unproductive.

9. Make Allowances for Times of Stress

If you're sick, or under an especially heavy work load, or if you are going through any rough period or recovery from psychological or physical stress, ease up on your program. Give yourself even more time to adjust to a new level or sleep longer than your scheduled level until things have calmed down and you are ready to return to the program. Obviously, you can't use every little upset or strain in life as an excuse to stay in bed longer or you'll never make any progress; but if there are truly unusual circumstances, make allowances for them. Someone with a bad cold needs more rest, and to ignore that need would be as foolish as trying, with that cold, to continue a vigorous exercise program. Or if you're going through a period when you're traveling, have an especially busy social schedule or are otherwise unable to keep regular hours, don't move to another level until you've established a more normal period of comfort.

You shouldn't be in any hurry, and if it takes the better part of a year to get from your present sleep time to the level you want to reach, that's fine. My own reduction program, which lowered my sleep needs from eight hours to six, took about five months. Yours may take more—or less.

Only you know what's going on in your mind and how you feel physically, and you have to tune the program to serve you. The targets and time spans offered here are suggestions only. If shorter or longer adjustment periods seem to work better for you—fine. Or if you are satisfied with just cutting out a half hour of sleep and want to stop there, that's a valid decision. This program is designed to leave you feeling well physically and pleased with the extra time you have gained. *It makes no sense to proceed if you don't feel well or if you decide you no longer want as much additional waking time.*

10. Take Advantage of Naps and Stress Reducers

Naps can be a tremendous help to some people in carrying out a sleep reduction program by offering at least two benefits. By relying on naps to supplement your shortened night sleep, you gain a lot of flexibility in your total sleep schedule. Many people will find that dropping from eight hours to six and a half becomes easier if they can sleep six hours at night and have a refreshing half-hour break in the middle of the day when they begin to sag. Furthermore, although it hasn't yet been proved in a sleep lab, nap time seems to be richer, more restorative, than night sleep for many people. A half-hour midday nap actually seems to do them as much good as an additional hour or more in bed in the morning or evening.

In fact, many people with really hectic schedules seem to thrive on short night sleep supplemented by naps. The prototype was Thomas Edison, whom we've already discussed. Winston Churchill was another famous napper. He said he tried whenever possible to get an hour's nap in the afternoon, and that twenty minutes, if he could do no better, would also renew him. Breaking up the day's routine, he added, was his way of doing a day and a half's work in one. President Harry Truman was another inveterate napper. He reported that whenever he felt tired he excused himself, even from a Cabinet meeting, to go and lie down "if only for five minutes." President Kennedy kept a full-sized bed on his plane, *Caroline,* so he could nap whenever his travel schedule got frenetic, especially during campaigns. An often-repeated nap story concerns the indefatigable Eleanor Roosevelt. She was to speak at a rally in Madison Square Garden but, when introduced, was found to be sound asleep in her chair on the podium. When she was awakened, she apologized and told her audience that she had become so accustomed to grabbing a few winks that whenever she felt the need she became oblivious of her surroundings or circumstances.

Not all of us have a ready opportunity to nap during the day. The boss may close the door and put his or her head on the desk, but woe to the rest of us caught napping on the job. For such people, Senator William Proxmire suggests a fifteen-minute-or-so snooze just before dinner.[3] And some may find that a half hour's nap immediately after dinner makes it possible for them to stay up an hour or more later than their usual bedtime. (One warning: if you nap too close to bedtime you'll most likely ruin your sleep.)

There are other people for whom naps simply don't work, at any time of the day. While affirming the recuperative value of naps, recent studies at the University of Pennsylvania—under the direction of Dr. Frederick J. Evans—have confirmed the fact that while all of us wake up a bit groggy from an afternoon nap, some people quickly recover and feel fine and others simply stay groggy, often for the rest of the day.[4]

If naps don't agree with you, there's nothing to do but forget them. But if you are a successful napper and find them revitalizing, by all means make use of them in your sleep program. There's no evidence that fifteen minutes of nap time is a substitute for an hour's sleep at night, but sleep researchers have noted enough people who do seem to benefit inordinately from naps to speculate about what these short periods might do for us. One study, headed by Dr. Ismet Karacan, who runs the sleep center at Baylor College of Medicine in Houston, concluded that short naps seem to be "refreshing out of proportion to their duration."[5]

So if naps are good *to* you—that is, if you are not allergic to them the way some people are—they are good *for* you. If you have worried that they might be a poor form of sleep because you can't pick up all the sleep stages you do in a ninety-minute cycle, or that they might somehow hurt your effort to cut back on total sleep time—stop worrying. They shouldn't hurt your nighttime sleep unless you nap too long or too often. In fact, they can be a major help in your sleep reduction program. However, your aim is to cut down your total sleep time, so be sure to add nap time to your night sleep when charting your progress.

Perhaps the value of naps lies not so much in the sleep they bring but in the relaxation they offer, as devices that break the day's tension. And there are other ways to dissipate stress. One is by doing the relaxation exercises discussed in Chapter 5, which can help you relax any time of the day and which may, in fact, ease you through a difficult period of adjustment to a new sleep plateau. Meditation, which quiets the body and clears the mind, is another stress-reducer that helps some people sleep fewer hours. Dr. Hartmann has reported that a "number of people" have told him they were able to get by on less sleep because of their meditation breaks and that, since they'd been meditating forty minutes a day, they slept one to two hours less.[6] In Dr. Hartmann's view, by reducing stress these people have lessened their need for REM-dreaming time, which means the last few hours of night sleep can be eliminated.

Some proponents of meditation have even made the outright claim that meditation induces a unique state that is so relaxing and restorative that those who practice it will surely need less sleep. But that's not a promise universally made by teachers of meditation. When Dr. Herbert Benson of the Harvard Medical School wrote his best-selling *The Relaxation Response,* he made no such claim: "Meditation is . . . not a form of sleep; nor can it be used as a substitute for sleep. Meditation evokes some of the physiological changes that are found in sleep, but the two are not in any way interchangeable, nor is one a substitute for the other. In fact, a look into the sleeping habits of meditators left us with reports that some slept more after regularly practicing meditation and others less. Some noted no change at all."[7]

It's also questionable as to whether meditation *is* a

unique state. In fact, one study that came out of the psychology department at the University of Washington in Seattle in 1976 was downright embarrassing to some meditators. A group of researchers there took five Transcendental Meditation practitioners, all with at least two and half years of meditation experience (four of them were teachers of the technique), and asked them to meditate in the lab for forty-minute sessions for eight days while hooked up to EEG machines. The result: thirty-nine percent of meditation time was spent in a state of wakefulness, nineteen percent in Stage One sleep, twenty-three percent in Stage Two and seventeen percent in Stages Three and Four. Even if Stage One were eliminated as a state of semisleep or "drowsiness," they spent forty percent of their meditation time asleep! These researchers could find no unique state in TM. As far as they were concerned, the meditators were just plain taking a nap and it was likely that "the beneficial effects reported for meditation are due to the sleep that occurs."[8]

In her excellent book *Freedom in Meditation,* Dr. Patricia Carrington, a clinical psychologist at Princeton, acknowledges that meditators often do drift off into a nap, but adds, "I have noticed that these brief naps that may occur during meditation seem to have a special subjective quality. People often report them as not feeling like sleep. They seem to have a more beneficial and alerting effect than a regular nap." She argues, too, that Stage One sleep is a very small part of the nightly sleep experience, but that in meditation this hovering between wakefulness and light sleep is sustained, perhaps providing much of meditation's value. She also notes that during meditation a person's brain waves have an "evenness and rhythmicity" that don't show up during normal sleep. And so on.[9]

The controversy continues, but one thing is clear: for whatever reason, meditation *does* reduce stress and increase the ability to cope with stress—there have been credible lab tests to prove it[10]—and that is all that matters. If meditation relaxes you so that you can handle a sleep reduction program better, by all means practice it. But be honest: if you are napping during part of your meditation period, add that nap time onto your total sleep time for the day.

11. If It Helps, Sleep One Half Hour Longer on Weekends

Many people who diet find it is easier to be strict during the week if they cheat a little on weekends. The same principle may work here. As we noted, the subjects of the San Diego–Irvine experiment said they felt they could have adjusted more easily if they had had a bit longer to sleep on weekends. This won't be true for everybody. Just as some dieters have to follow their diet religiously every day because a single slip throws them back into sinful ways, so some sleepers may find an extra half hour on weekends destroys the momentum they have built up during the week. So this is a device to use only if you honestly think it will help you. *But no more than a half hour:* you do have to establish a rhythm and regularity to your sleep habits, and if you start to sleep really longer on Saturdays and Sundays, you will find adjustment to each new level much more difficult.

12. Give Yourself Some Rewards for Success

While you may want to cut your sleep time in order to have more hours to work, I think most people have to throw in some pleasure incentives as well, if they're to keep to their resolve. If you sleep one and a half hours less and you are glad to have an extra hour to moonlight, sift through your briefcase or do household chores, can't you take a half hour to read a book or enjoy a hobby or just chat with friends and loved ones? Freeing up time is meant to *reduce* pressures, not fill up every additional minute with still more "things to do." It won't be true for everyone, but without that pleasure bonus, most of us could easily end up resenting the whole idea so much we scuttle the program, or put ourselves in a very bitter frame of mind. What's more, fun periods perk you up. If you're a train commuter, have you ever noticed how many people sleep but never those who have looked forward to their bridge game? Look upon sleep reduction as a positive response to a fuller, more rewarding lifestyle. That, don't forget, is the point of the whole program.

13. Develop Good Sleep Habits

Since six hours of good sleep are worth more recuperatively than eight hours of light and disturbed sleep, improving the quality or efficiency of your sleep can be a major support to your reduction effort. You've noted the difference yourself many times—how much more rested you feel when you can say, "I slept like a log." Earlier, in Chapter 5, we looked at ways to improve sleep quality. Review and use them. The most important was already raised to the status of a rule: regularity of sleeping hours. Be sure also that your bedroom isn't too warm, that your bed is comfortable, that outside noise is muffled. Regular exercise contributes to sound sleep. So does a late-night routine that conditions you to sleep expectations. Avoid sleeping pills, but do have a light snack before going to bed if you're hungry. These measures can be especially reassuring at a time when you are trying to change the sleep routine of your lifetime and when you may well be feeling some apprehension about these changes and the loss of accustomed sleep.

14. Make Your Sleep Reduction Program Part of a Reevaluation of Your Lifestyle

Stressed throughout this book is the concept that sleep must be viewed as just one aspect of the whole person. The soundness of our sleep and our sleep needs are reflections of our personalities and the way we organize our world. We know the amount of sleep we get affects how we feel physically and psychologically, and how we take care of ourselves physically and psychologically also affects the amount of sleep we'll be comfortable with. We've seen that troubled individuals seem to need more sleep and that those who exercise and keep fit seem to need less. People who eat too much, drink too much and get no exercise won't get very far with this sleep reduction program either. Nor will those who have no real sense of the value of time, of how by expanding it we gain opportunities that would otherwise be lost to us. Undertaking a sleep reduction program becomes perforce a commitment to review, and perhaps reorganize, our entire lifestyle.

Those who have trained themselves to sleep fewer hours are in command of themselves and success-oriented. You really have to start thinking of yourself that way, too. You are ready to give up sleep in order to do more, experience more, achieve more. It takes resolve, motivation; you have to pull yourself together. And then as you do sleep fewer hours and find additional time to accomplish more, your life becomes richer and you become more interesting, pleased with yourself and, in all likelihood, motivated to do still more.

In short, since changing your lifelong sleep habits requires a major adjustment in the way you live, it is a very good time to reconsider just how you *do* live.

*   *   *

And that is it—a sleep reduction program that is uncomplicated, responsible and sensible. It is based on the premise that most people who really want to reduce their sleeping hours can do so, if they do it gradually and moderately and listen to what their bodies and minds are telling them along the way. In exchange for the temporary distress of adjustment, they gain something that is very precious—time. More time, more hours awake, is a gift of more life. And that gift is yours for the taking.

APPENDIX I

A List of Sleep Disorder Centers

We cannot reduce sleep length if our sleep is disturbed and inefficient. A sleep reduction program should be a voluntary effort, not a shortening dictated by insomnia or other problems.

In the 1970s a growing number of clinics were established to help people who have sleep difficulties. While insomnia is the most prevalent complaint, these clinics also help those who suffer from uncontrollable daytime sleepiness (narcolepsy), nighttime respiratory problems, frequent nightmares, sleepwalking and other troubles. Treatment must start with diagnosis, and that may require spending several nights at a clinic for study of sleep patterns. Clinics may require referral by your own physician.

The following list of clinics in the United States and Canada, arranged alphabetically by city name, was supplied by the American Association of Sleep Disorder Centers.

Sleep Disorders Center
Baltimore City Hospital
4940 Eastern Avenue
Baltimore, Maryland 21224
(301) 396-5859
Contact: Richard Allen, M.D.

Sleep Disorders Clinic
Boston Children's Hospital
300 Longwood Avenue
Boston, Massachusetts 02115
(617) 734-6000
Contact: Myron Belfer, M.D.

Sleep-Wake Disorders Unit
Montefiore Hospital
111 East 210th Street
Bronx, New York 10467
(212) 920-4841
Contact: Charles Pollak, M.D.

Sleep Disorders Center
Department of Neurology
Crozer Chester Medical Center
15th Street and Upland Avenue
Chester, Pennsylvania 19013
(215) 874-1184
Contact: Calvin Stafford, M.D.

Sleep Disorders Center
Suite 214, Wesley Pavilion
Northwestern University Medical Center
250 East Superior Street
Chicago, Illinois 60611
(312) 649-8649
Contact: John Cayaffa, M.D.

Sleep Disorders Center
Rush-Presbyterian-St. Luke's
1753 West Congress Parkway
Chicago, Illinois 60612
(312) 942-5000
Contact: Rosalind Cartwright, Ph.D.

Sleep Disorders Center
23 Mont Reid Pavillion
Cincinnati General Hospital
Cincinnati, Ohio 45267
(513) 861-3100
Contact: Milton Kramer, M.D.

Sleep Disorders Center
Mt. Sinai Hospital
University Circle
1800 East 105th Street
Cleveland, Ohio 44106
(216) 795-6000
Contact: Herbert Weiss, M.D.

Sleep Disorders Center
Department of Psychiatry
St. Luke's Hospital
11311 Shaker Boulevard
Cleveland, Ohio 44104
(216) 368-7000
Contact: Joel Steinberg, M.D.

Sleep Clinic
Department of Psychiatry
Ohio State University
473 West 12th Street
Columbus, Ohio 43210
(614) 422-5982
Contact: Helmut Schmidt, M.D.

Sleep Disorders Center
Henry Ford Hospital
2799 West Grand Boulevard
Detroit, Michigan 48202
(313) 876-2223
Contact: Thomas Roth, Ph.D.

Sleep Disorders Clinic
Department of Psychiatry
Dartmouth-Hitchcock Mental Health Center
2 Maynard Street
Hanover, New Hampshire 03755
(603) 646-2213
Contact: Peter Hauri, Ph.D.

Sleep Clinic
Baylor College of Medicine
1200 Moursand Street
Houston, Texas 77030
(713) 790-4886
Contact: Ismet Karacan, M.D.

Sleep Laboratory
Department of Anatomy
University of Arkansas Medical Center
4301 West Markham Street
Little Rock, Arkansas 72201
(501) 661-5272
Contact: Edgar Lucas, Ph.D.

Sleep Disorders Center
Baptist Memorial Hospital
899 Madison Avenue
Memphis, Tennessee 38146
(901) 522-5651
Contact: Helio Lemmi, M.D.

Sleep Disorders Center
Mt. Sinai Medical Center
4300 Alton Road
Miami Beach, Florida 33140
(305) 674-2385
Contact: Marvin Sackner, M.D.

Sleep Disorders Center
Neurology Department
Hennepin County Medical Center
701 Park Avenue
Minneapolis, Minnesota 55415
(612) 347-2121
Contact: Milton Ettinger, M.D.

Sleep Disorders Clinic
Hôpital du Sacré-Coeur
5400 Ouest, Boulevard Gouin
Montreal, Quebec, Canada H4J 1C5
(514) 333-2070
Contact: Jacques Montplaisir, M.D.

Sleep Disorders Center
Medical Sciences Buildings
New Jersey Medical School
100 Bergen Street
Newark, New Jersey 07103
(201) 456-4300
Contact: James Minard, Ph.D.

Sleep Disorders Center
Psychiatry and Neurology Department
Tulane Medical School
1432 Tulane Avenue
New Orleans, Louisiana 70112
(504) 588-5236
Contact: John Goethe, M.D.

Sleep Disorders Center
Presbyterian Hospital
Northeast 13th Street at Lincoln Boulevard
Oklahoma City, Oklahoma 73104
(405) 271-6312
Contact: William Orr, Ph.D.

Sleep Disorders Center
University of California–Irvine Medical Center
101 City Drive South
Orange, California 92688
(714) 634-5777
Contact: Jon Sassin, M.D.

Sleep Disorders Center
Ottawa General Hospital
43 Bruyère
Ottawa, Canada K1N 4C8
(613) 231-4738
Contact: Roger Broughton, M.D.

Sleep Disorders Center
Western Psychiatric Institute
3811 O'Hara Street
Pittsburgh, Pennsylvania 15261
(412) 624-2246
Contact: David Kupfer, M.D.

Sleep Disorders Center
Suite 1402, 1260 15th Street
Santa Monica, California 90404
(213) 451-3270
Contact: John Beck, M.D.

Sleep Disorders Center
Stanford University Medical Center
Stanford, California 94305
(415) 497-7458
Contact: Laughton Miles, M.D.

Sleep Laboratory
Department of Psychiatry
State University of New York
Stony Brook, New York 11794
(516) 444-2069
Contact: Merrill M. Mitler, Ph.D.

Sleep Laboratory
Department of Neurology
University of Massachusetts Medical Center
55 Lake Avenue North
Worcester, Massachusetts 01605
(617) 856-3081
Contact: Sheldon Kapen, M.D.

Additional Sources of Help

The following clinics are not able to treat all sleep disorders but may be able to help you with your particular problem. (Again, the list is arranged alphabetically by city name.)

Department of Psychiatry
Albany Medical College of Union University
75 New Scotland Avenue
Albany, New York 12208
(518) 445-6851 or 445-6771
Contact: Vincenzo Castaldo, M.D.

Center for Developmental and Learning Disorders
Box 1190, Neurosciences
University of Alabama
7th Avenue South and 18th Street
Birmingham, Alabama 35294
(205) 934-3421
Contact: Vernon Pegram, Ph.D.

Sleep Clinic
Peter Bent Brigham Hospital and New Center
    of Psychotherapies
721 Huntington Avenue
Boston, Massachusetts 02115
(617) 732-6750 or 732-6628
Contact: Quentin Regestein, M.D.

Department of Medicine
Pulmonary Section
University of Texas Medical Branch
Unit 5C, Old John Sealy Hospital
Galveston, Texas 77550
(713) 765-2436
Contact: Michael Anch, Ph.D., or
John Remmers, M.D.

Sleep Facility
Clinical Psychophysiology Lab (116–A1)
Audie Murphy Memorial Veterans Administration
Hospital and University of Texas Medical
School
7400 Merton Minter Boulevard
San Antonio, Texas 78284
(512) 696-9660
Contact: Augustin de la Pena, Ph.D.

Sleep Disorders Clinic
Department of Psychiatry
Veterans Administration Hospital.
3350 La Jolla Village Drive
San Diego, California 92161
(714) 453-7500
Contact: Daniel F. Kripke, M.D.

Clarke Institute of Psychiatry
250 College Street
Toronto, Ontario, Canada M5T 1R8
(416) 979-2221
Contact: Harvey Moldofsky, M.D.

APPENDIX II
Your Sleep Log: A Model

Keeping a daily log during your sleep reduction program is essential for a number of reasons: to keep accurate track of your total sleep time, to reinforce the discipline of daily accounting, as a reference to gain perspective on your progress, and as a supportive outlet for your feelings during trying transition days. But you are sleeping less to gain time, not lose it in writing long diary essays. This form should make the daily entries easier and quicker. Type it out and duplicate it, or simply use it as an example of the kind of checklist you can create yourself to monitor how well you're doing.

Date _____

Time to sleep _____

Time up _____

      Total hours night sleep _____

Nap time _____

    TOTAL HOURS OF SLEEP _____

Quality of sleep:
    ☐ great ☐ good ☐ restless but adequate
    ☐ unsatisfactory

Morning State:
    ☐ rested and refreshed ☐ just okay
    ☐ really groggy
    ☐ could hardly get out of bed

Energy level during day:
☐ good all day
☐ good in morning, sagged in afternoon
☐ poor in morning, picked up in afternoon
☐ tired all day

Functional capacity (ability to concentrate, reaction to pressure, creativity, etc.):
☐ peak levels ☐ average day
☐ okay but below par ☐ inadequate

Emotional state:
☐ especially cheerful, optimistic
☐ average day ☐ below-average day
☐ depressed, out of it

Evening state:
☐ fine until bedtime ☐ tired but functional
☐ very tired, couldn't wait until bedtime
☐ fell asleep after dinner

Physical state:
☐ fine ☐ thoroughly exhausted
☐ had some problems (note:) _____

Additional observations: _____
_____
_____
_____

NOTES

Introduction

1. Conversation with Dr. Kleitman. (Hereafter, whenever a direct quotation is not footnoted, it can be assumed the quotation was derived from an interview.)

2. Dr. Hartmann's views are most easily accessible in his paperback book, *The Functions of Sleep* (New Haven: Yale University Press, 1973). Pages 53–70 cover the question of personality traits of long and short sleepers, while pages 71–81 deal with sleep length variations triggered by emotional states. Hartmann's views on the former subject are controversial. Dr. Wilse B. Webb of the University of Florida has conducted surveys that find no correlation between sleep length and personality: see Wilse B. Webb and Janette Friel, "Sleep Stage and Personality Characteristics of 'Natural' Long and Short Sleepers," *Science,* Vol. 171 (February 12, 1971), pp. 587–88. Of subsequent studies, two uphold Hartmann (one was conducted by Hartmann with Cheryl Spinweber, "Long and Short Sleepers: Male and Female Subjects," *Sleep Research,* Vol. 5 [1976], p. 112; and the other by Donald Stuss *et al.,* "Personality and Performance Measures in Natural Extreme Short Sleepers," *Sleep Research,* Vol. 4 [1975], p. 204), and one strongly supports Webb (Robert A. Hicks and Robert J. Pellegrini, "Anxiety Levels of Short and Long Sleepers," *Psychological Reports,* Vol. 41 [1977], pp. 569–70).

Chapter 1

1. Both the AMA and Blue Cross/Blue Shield ads were based on two studies. The first was conducted by the American Cancer Society, and reported in E. Cuyler Hammond, "Some Preliminary Findings on Physical Complaints from a Prospective Study of 1,064,004 Men and Women," *American Journal of Public Health,* Vol. 54 (January 1964), pp. 11–23, and in E. Cuyler Hammond and Lawrence Garfinkel, "Coronary Heart Disease, Stroke and Aortic Aneurysm," *Archives of Environmental Health,* Vol. 19 (1969), pp. 167–82. This study, based on questionnaires sent to men and women in twenty-five states and on a follow-up six years later, showed that those who sleep more than eight hours were more likely to die from heart disease, stroke or aortic aneurysm.

The second study was based on a poll of 7,000 residents of Alameda County, California, and conducted by the State Department of Public Health with the assistance of Dr. Lester Breslow, dean of the School of Public Health at UCLA. It was reported in Nedra B. Belloc and Lester Breslow, "Relationship of Physical Health Status and Health Practices," *Preventive Medicine,* Vol. 1 (1972), pp. 409–21, and in Belloc's "Relationship of Health Practices and Mortality," *Preventive Medicine,* Vol. 2 (1973), pp. 67–81. This poll correlated health with living habits and found that both those who sleep nine hours or more and those—particularly men—who sleep six hours or less are not as healthy as seven- to eight-hour sleepers.

And yet, when people who sleep far less than six hours are brought into sleep labs for physical examinations and psychological testing, they prove to be perfectly healthy. How does one explain the contradiction?

First of all, the data are suspect. The statistics are based on questionnaires, not interviews, and people usually don't bother to average out their irregular sleep hours. Health-conscious people tend to err in favor of what they believe is the "proper" amount of sleep.

Secondly, it is not clear what is cause and what is effect. People can certainly sleep more or less because they are ill, or frail enough to be predisposed to illness. As Belloc admits, "Illness may cause insomnia or a need for more sleep, rather than the reverse" (". . . Mortality," p. 73).

Nor do the studies differentiate among short sleepers. There are short sleepers who are normal, healthy and comfortable with the sleep they are getting. And there are short sleepers who are forced to sleep less because of pressures, who are therefore tired and under stress —which, of course, takes its toll on the body. If stress is causing insomnia—and especially if the person takes sleeping pills to help the insomnia and "pep" pills to help get through the day—the medical problems are obviously exacerbated.

Nevertheless, the program presented in this book, as you will see, does not recommend that most people cut their sleep time below six hours. If seven hours of sleep is recommended, it is hard to believe, given probability curves, that six hours can have even long-term detrimental effects. Moreover, this program stresses that those undertaking it find a level of sleep at which they are rested and comfortable, and that if they continue to feel tired at any level they should go back to a level of sleeping hours at which they *are* rested and comfortable.

2. "Big Changes in How People Live—New Official Look," *U.S. News & World Report,* January 16, 1978, p. 42.

3. Jonathan and Marianna Kastner, *Sleep: The Mysterious Third of Your Life* (New York: Harcourt, Brace & World, 1968), pp. 82–83.

4. Gay Gaer Luce and Julius Segal, "What Time Is

It? The Body's Clock Knows," *The New York Times Magazine,* April 13, 1966, p. 30.

5. Ian Oswald, *Sleeping and Waking* (Amsterdam, N.Y.: Elsevier Publishing Co., 1962), p. 172.

6. "On Sleep: The Long and the Short of It," August 22, 1975, p. 31.

7. William C. Dement, *Some Must Watch While Some Must Sleep* (Stanford, Cal.: Stanford Alumni Association, 1972), p. 4.

8. *Sleep and Wakefulness,* revised edition (Chicago: University of Chicago Press, 1963), p. 120.

9. *Ibid.,* p. 114. There is an excellent summary of sleep variations at different ages in Wilse B. Webb, *Sleep: The Gentle Tyrant* (Englewood Cliffs, N.J.: Prentice-Hall, Inc., 1975), pp. 28–38.

10. *The Sleep Disorders* (Kalamazoo, Mich.: The Upjohn Co., 1977), p. 17.

11. *Ibid.,* p. 14.

12. Maggie Scarf, "Oh, for a Decent Night's Sleep!", *The New York Times Magazine,* October 21, 1973, p. 80.

13. Dement, *op. cit.*

14. Doris Kearns, *Lyndon Johnson and the American Dream* (New York: Signet Books, 1977), p. 185. See also Richard Harwood and Haynes Johnson, *Lyndon* (New York: Praeger Publishers, 1973), p. 129.

15. Vernon Louviere, "How the President Stays Healthy," *Nation's Business,* September 1978, p. 44.

16. "A Tired Jimmy," *Newsweek,* November 13, 1978, p. 55.

17. July 1, 1977, p. 1. The other information was provided during a phone interview.

18. Wilse B. Webb, "Did Edison Invent Non-Sleep, Too?", *Sleep Forum* ("letter" issued by the Department of Psychiatry, University of Texas, Dallas), 1978, pp. 26–27. See also Israel Bram, "How Much Sleep Do You Need?", *Medical Record* (N.Y.), Vol. 150 (September 20, 1939), p. 219: "Thomas A. Edison wrote

me in 1927 that up to the sixtieth year of life he slept four hours daily, but afterward, he increased his sleep to six."

19. *The Sleep Instinct* (London: Routledge & Kegan Paul, 1977), p. 124.

20. "Two Cases of Healthy Insomnia," *Electroencephalography and Clinical Neurophysiology,* Vol. 24 (1968), pp. 378–80.

21. Meddis *et al.,* "An Extreme Case of Healthy Insomnia," *Electroencephalography and Clinical Neurophysiology,* Vol. 35 (1973), pp. 213–14.

22. Stuss *et al.,* see Introduction, note 2.

23. Gay Gaer Luce and Julius Segal, *Sleep* (New York: Coward-McCann, Inc., 1966), p. 263.

24. Nino Lo Bello, "Italian Farmer Says He Has Not Slept for 20 Years, 'Travels' World," *Sacramento Bee,* October 12, 1970, n.p.; "Retired Italian Farmer Stays Awake 30 Years," *GRIT,* July 20, 1977, n.p.

25. *Sleep: The Gentle Tyrant,* p. 67.

26. Yvonne Dunleavy, "How to Get Along on Less Sleep," *New York Sunday News,* June 8, 1975, p. 18.

27. "Are You Getting Enough Sleep? Interview with Dr. Richard Wyatt, National Institute of Mental Health," *U.S. News & World Report,* October 16, 1972, p. 48.

Chapter 2

1. Bram, see Chapter 1, note 18, p. 221.

2. Dement, see Chapter 1, note 7, p. 13.

3. Scarf, see Chapter 1, note 12, p. 71.

4. Dement, *op. cit.,* p. 25.

5. Webb, see Chapter 1, note 9, p. 141.

6. *Ibid.* Webb is citing two studies: Calvin S. Hall and Robert L. Van de Castle, *The Content Analysis of Dreams* (New York: Appleton-Century-Crofts, 1966), and Fred Snyder, "The Phenomenology of Dreaming,"

in *The Psychodynamic Implications of the Physiological Studies on Dreams,* ed. Leo Madow and Laurence H. Snow (Springfield, Ill.: Charles C Thomas, 1970).

7. Hall and Van de Castle, p. 181.

8. Dement, *op. cit.,* p. 50.

9. Nathaniel Kleitman, "Basic Rest-Activity Cycle in Relation to Sleep and Wakefulness," in *Sleep: Physiology & Pathology,* ed. Anthony Kales (Philadelphia: J. B. Lippincott Co., 1969), p. 37.

10. Lee Edson, "Bad Day at the Office?", *Think,* July/August, 1977, p. 33.

11. *Ibid.*

12. Webb, *op. cit.,* p. 129.

13. D. J. Mullaney *et al.,* "Sleep During and After Gradual Sleep Reduction," *Psychophysiology,* Vol. 14 (May 1977), p. 241.

Chapter 3

1. Rosalind Dymond Cartwright, *A Primer on Sleep and Dreaming* (Reading, Mass.: Addison-Wesley Publishing Co., 1978), pp. 83–84.

2. Quoted in Jody Gaylin, "The Way We Sleep Is the Way We Live," *Psychology Today,* May 1977, p. 32.

3. Patrick Young, "Dreams Set Your Mood," *The National Observer,* June 20, 1977, p. 1.

4. "The Effect of Dream Deprivation," *Science,* Vol. 131 (June 10, 1960), p. 1705.

5. Gerald W. Vogel, "REM Deprivation: Dreaming and Psychosis," *Archives of General Psychiatry,* Vol. 18 (March 1968), p. 313.

6. *Ibid.,* p. 314.

7. Dement, see Chapter 1, note 7, p. 91.

8. David Foulkes, "Sleep," *Encyclopedia Britannica,* 15th ed. (Chicago: Encyclopedia Britannica, Inc., 1974), Vol. 16, p. 881.

9. Meddis, see Chapter 1, note 19, p. 76.

10. Dement, *op. cit.*, p. 30.

11. David Foulkes, *The Psychology of Sleep* (New York: Charles Scribner's Sons, 1966), p. 176.

12. Vogel, *op. cit.*, p. 327.

13. Meddis, *op. cit.*, pp. 66–67.

14. Douglas Colligan, "The Sleep-Starvation Cure," *New York,* December 5, 1977, p. 91.

15. Wolfgang Dühringer *et al.*, "Clinical Implications of Sleep Deprivation Therapy on Affective Disorders," *Sleep Research,* Vol. 4 (1975), p. 243.

16. Meddis, *op. cit.*, p. 67.

17. John H. Herman *et al.*, "The Problem of NREM Dream Recall Re-examined," in *The Mind in Sleep: Psychology and Psychophysiology,* ed. A. Arkin, J. Antrobus and S. Ellman (Hillsdale, N.J.: Lawrence Erlbaum Associates, 1978), p. 64.

18. Webb, see Chapter 1, note 9, p. 131. Also Mullaney *et al.*, see Chapter 2, note 13, p. 241.

19. Vogel, *op. cit.*, p. 320.

Chapter 4

1. Webb, see Chapter 1, note 9, p. 120.

2. *Ibid.*

3. *Ibid.*, p. 121.

4. *Ibid.*, p. 126.

5. E. J. P. Caille *et al.*, "Loss of Sleep and Combat Efficiency: Effects of the Work/Rest Cycle," in *Aspects of Human Efficiency: Diurnal Rhythm and Loss of Sleep,* ed. W. P. Colquhoun (London: The English Universities Press, Ltd., 1972), p. 189.

6. Luce and Segal, see Chapter 1, note 23, pp. 90–92.

7. Dement, see Chapter 1, note 7, pp. 8–12.

8. Robert O. Pasnau *et al.*, "The Psychological Effects of 205 Hours of Sleep Deprivation," *Archives of General Psychiatry,* Vol. 18 (April 1968), pp. 501–2.

9. Walter R. Gove, "Sleep Deprivation: A Cause of Psychotic Disorganization," *American Journal of Sociology,* Vol. 75 (March 1970), p. 789.

10. Webb, *op. cit.,* p. 126.

11. J. A. C. Brown, *Techniques of Persuasion* (Baltimore: Penguin Books, 1972), pp. 267–93.

12. Hartmann, see Introduction, note 2, p. 41.

13. Dement, *op. cit.,* note 7, p. 3.

14. Joann S. Lublin, "Perchance to Dream: Sleep-Disorder Clinics Grow as Researchers Work Out Treatments," *The Wall Street Journal,* January 11, 1978, p. 1.

15. Dement, *op. cit.,* p. 19.

16. Meddis, see Chapter 1, note 19, p. 126.

17. *Ibid.,* Preface.

18. Scarf, see Chapter 1, note 12, p. 82.

19. Dement, *op. cit.,* p. 16.

20. Luce and Segal, *op. cit.,* note 23, pp. 174–75.

21. Meddis, *op. cit.,* p. 6.

22. Hartmann, *op. cit.,* p. 147.

23. "Sleep for the Memory," *Time,* August 27, 1976, p. 39.

24. Hartmann, *op. cit.,* p. 97.

25. "Are Stages of Sleep Related to Waking Behavior?", *American Scientist,* Vol. 61 (May-June 1973), p. 335.

26. Truett Allison and Henry Van Twyver, "The Evolution of Sleep," *Natural History,* February 1970, p. 63.

27. Meddis, *op. cit.,* p. 15.

28. *Ibid.,* p. 32.

29. Dement, *op. cit.,* p. 16.

30. "Sleep Duration and Feeling State," *International Psychiatry Clinics,* Vol. 7 (1970), p. 83.

31. Kastner, see Chapter 1, note 3, pp. 98–99.

Chapter 5

1. "Solving the Mystery of Sleep," *Science Digest,* August 1967, p. 44.

2. Hauri, see Chapter 1, note 10, p. 26.

3. "How Much Sleep Do You Need? Interview with Dr. Julius Segal, National Institute of Mental Health," *U.S. News & World Report,* December 28, 1970, p. 34.

4. *How to Sleep Better: A Drug-Free Program for Overcoming Insomnia* (Englewood Cliffs, N.J.: Prentice-Hall, Inc., 1977), p. 127.

5. Edwin Diamond, "Long Day's Journey Into the Insomniac's Night," *The New York Times Magazine,* October 1, 1967, p. 108.

6. Webb, see Chapter 1, note 9, p. 46.

7. *Ibid.*

8. "The Effects of Changing the Phase and Duration of Sleep," *Journal of Experimental Psychology,* Vol. 7 (1976), p. 38.

9. Ellen Switzer and George Langmyhr, "Your Sex Life and How It Affects the Way You Sleep," *Vogue,* August 1973, pp. 120–21, 148. See also Julius Segal, "How Do You Feel After Sex—Sleepy or Exhilarated? You May Be Fooling Yourself," *Glamour,* May 1978, pp. 78, 86.

10. Hauri, *op. cit.,* p. 26.

11. Ernest Hartmann, "L-Tryptophan—The Sleeping Pill of the Future?", *Psychology Today,* December 1978, p. 180.

12. Harold M. Schmeck, Jr., "U.S. Study of Sleep Drugs Finds Risks and Overuse," *The New York Times,* April 5, 1979, p. 1.

13. Merrill M. Mitler *et al.,* "Sleeplessness, Sleep Attacks and Things That Go Wrong in the Night," *Psychology Today,* December 1975, p. 46.

14. Hauri, *op. cit.,* p. 25.

15. Scarf, see Chapter 1, note 12, p. 80.

16. Richard Trubo, "The Complete Sleep Book," *Good Housekeeping*, March 1978, p. 77.

17. Emma Lewis, "How to Get a Good Night's Sleep," *Harper's Bazaar*, September 1973, p. 109.

18. Dement, see Chapter 1, note 7, p. 82.

19. Mitler *et al.*, pp. 45–46.

20. Meddis, see Chapter 1, note 19, pp. 104–5.

Chapter 6

1. Edson, see Chapter 2, note 10, p. 33. See also Barbara Kleban, "Dr. Franz Halberg Measures the Body's Natural Cycles (But Please Don't Call Them Biorhythms)," *People*, November 6, 1978, p. 123.

2. Frank A. Brown, Jr., "Periodicity, Biological," *Encyclopedia Britannica*, 15th ed. (Chicago: Encyclopedia Britannica, Inc., 1974), Vol. 14, p. 72.

3. *Ibid.*, p. 73.

4. Kastner, see Chapter 1, note 3, p. 84.

5. Kleitman, see Chapter 1, note 8, pp. 178–81.

6. Kleban, *op. cit.*, p. 125.

7. Kleitman, *op. cit.*, p. 182.

8. Wilse B. Webb and H. W. Agnew, Jr., "The Effects of a Chronic Limitation of Sleep Length," *Psychophysiology*, Vol. 11 (1974), p. 273.

9. Robert Ogilvie and Sidney Segalowitz, "The Effect of 20% Sleep Reduction Upon Mood, Learning and Performance Measures," *Sleep Research*, Vol. 4 (1975), p. 242.

10. Laverne C. Johnson and William L. MacLeod, "Sleep and Awake Behavior During Gradual Sleep Reduction," *Perceptual and Motor Skills*, Vol. 36 (1973), p. 95.

11. Mullaney *et al.*, see Chapter 2, note 13, p. 243.

12. Friedmann *et al.*, "Performance and Mood During and After Gradual Sleep Reduction," *Psychophysiology*, Vol. 14 (May 1977), p. 249.

13. *Ibid.,* p. 248.

14. *Ibid.,* p. 249.

15. *Ibid.*

16. *Ibid.,* p. 248.

17. *Ibid.,* p. 249.

18. *Ibid.*

19. Mullaney *et al., op. cit.,* p. 243.

20. Friedmann *et al., op. cit.,* p. 249.

Chapter 7

1. Mullaney *et al.,* see Chapter 2, note 13, p. 244.

2. Hartmann, see Introduction, note 2, p. 69.

3. *You Can Do It! Senator Proxmire's Exercise, Diet and Relaxation Plan* (New York: Simon & Schuster, 1973), p. 228.

4. Frederick J. Evans *et al.,* "Sleep Patterns in Replacement and Appetitive Nappers," paper presented at the American Psychological Association, Washington, D.C., September 1976, p. 10.

5. Ismet Karacan *et al.,* "The Effects of Naps on Nocturnal Sleep: Influence on the Need for Stage-1, REM and Stage-4 Sleep," *Biological Psychiatry,* Vol. 2 (1970), p. 396.

6. Hartmann, *op. cit.,* p. 77.

7. New York: William Morrow and Co., 1975, pp. 64–65.

8. Robert R. Pagano *et al.,* "Sleep During Transcendental Meditation," *Science,* Vol. 191 (January 1976), p. 309.

9. Garden City, N.Y.: Anchor Press/Doubleday, 1978, pp. 47–48.

10. Chiefly those of Herbert Benson at Harvard and R. Keith Wallace at the University of California at Los Angeles, reported in Benson, pp. 59–68, and Carrington, pp. 49–51.

BIBLIOGRAPHY

The reader interested in learning more about sleep is fortunate, for there are two books still in print that are short but packed with information and inexpensive, since they are paperbacks: Wilse B. Webb's *Sleep: The Gentle Tyrant,* published by Prentice-Hall in 1975, and William C. Dement's *Some Must Watch While Some Must Sleep,* published by the Stanford Alumni Association in 1972. Webb's title is taken from Dr. Johnson and Dement's from Shakespeare, so you know you will be learning from men who can put technical knowledge in human terms.

"Age, Health Affect Sleep Patterns," *Today's Health,* November 1968, p. 77.

Allison, Truett, and Henry Van Twyver, "The Evolution of Sleep," *Natural History,* February 1970, pp. 56–65.

"Are You Getting Enough Sleep? Interview with Dr. Richard Wyatt, National Institute of Mental Health," *U.S. News & World Report,* October 16, 1972, pp. 45–48.

Belloc, Nedra B., "Relationship of Health Practices and Mortality," *Preventive Medicine,* Vol. 2 (1973), pp. 67–81.

—— and Lester Breslow, "Relationship of Physical Health Status and Health Practices," *Preventive Medicine,* Vol. 1 (1972), pp. 409–21.

Benson, Herbert, *The Relaxation Response.* New York: William Morrow and Co., 1975.

"The Better Way: Practical Help for People with Sleeping Problems," *Good Housekeeping,* May 1974, pp. 169–70.

"Biophysical Sleep Control for Astronauts," *Space World,* February 1975, pp. 28–29.

Blau, Eleanor, "Bronx Unit Helps Sleepless to Sleep and Those Asleep to Wake Up," *The New York Times,* October 22, 1977, pp. 23, 35.

Brady, Kathleen, "Sleep: How Much Do You Really Need?", *Working Woman,* November 1976, pp. 60–61.

Bram, Israel, "How Much Sleep Do You Need?", *Medical Record* (N.Y.), Vol. 150 (September 20, 1939), pp. 219–22.

Brody, Jane E., "Personal Health: Sleeping Pills May Aggravate the Very Problem They Are Supposed to Be Solving," *The New York Times,* April 11, 1979, p. C10.

Brothers, Dr. Joyce, "The Need for Sleep and Dreams," *Good Housekeeping,* November 1970, pp. 54–56.

Brown, Frank A., Jr., "Periodicity, Biological," *Encyclopedia Britannica,* 15th edition (Chicago: Encyclopedia Britannica, Inc., 1974), Vol. 14, pp. 69–75.

Brown, J. A. C., *Techniques of Persuasion.* Baltimore: Penguin Books, 1972.

Burns, John, "The Fondness for Naps Persists in Maoist China," *The New York Times,* September 30, 1973, p. 16.

Caille, E. J. P., A. M. C. Quideau, J. F. J. Girard, J. C. Gubar, and A. C. Monteil, "Loss of Sleep and Combat Efficiency: Effects of the Work/Rest Cycle," in *Aspects of Human Efficiency: Diurnal Rhythm and Loss of Sleep,* ed. W. P. Colquhoun (London: The English Universities Press, Ltd., 1972), pp. 177–91.

Carrington, Patricia, *Freedom in Meditation.* Garden City, New York: Anchor Press/Doubleday, 1978.

Cartwright, Rosalind Dymond, "Happy Endings for Our Dreams," *Psychology Today,* December 1978, pp. 66–76.

——, *Night Life: Explorations in Dreaming.* Englewood Cliffs, N.J.: Prentice-Hall, Inc., 1977.

——, *A Primer on Sleep and Dreaming.* Reading, Mass.: Addison-Wesley Publishing Co., 1978.

Chase-Marshall, Janet, "Larks and Owls: Some People Are as Different as Day and Night," *VIVA,* December 1977, pp. 57, 94–98.

Cherry, Laurence, "A New Vision of Dreams," *The New York Times Magazine,* July 3, 1977, pp. 9–13, 34.

Coates, Thomas, and Carl Thoresen, *How to Sleep Better: A Drug-Free Program for Overcoming Insomnia.* Englewood Cliffs, N.J.: Prentice-Hall, Inc., 1977.

Colligan, Douglas, "The Sleep-Starvation Cure," *New York,* December 5, 1977, pp. 84–92.

Current Research on Sleep and Dreams. Washington, D.C.: U.S. Department of Health, Education and Welfare (Public Health Service Publication #1389), 1966.

Dement, William C., "The Biological Role of REM Sleep (Circa 1968)," in *Sleep: Physiology & Pathology,* ed. Anthony Kales (Philadelphia: J. B. Lippincott Co., 1969), pp. 245–65.

——, "The Effect of Dream Deprivation," *Science,* Vol. 131 (June 10, 1960), pp. 1705–7.

——, *Some Must Watch While Some Must Sleep.* Stanford, Cal.: Stanford Alumni Association, 1972.

—— and Stephen Greenberg, "Changes in Total Amount of Stage Four Sleep as a Function of Partial Sleep Deprivation," *Electroencephalography and Clinical Neurophysiology,* Vol. 20 (1966), pp. 523–26.

Diamond, Edwin, "Long Day's Journey Into the Insomniac's Night," *The New York Times Magazine,* October 1, 1967, pp. 30, 106–16.

"Dream More to Remember Better," *Science News,* Vol. 110 (August 28, 1976), p. 135.

Dühringer, Wolfgang, Anna Wirz-Justice, and Günter Hole, "Clinical Implications of Sleep Deprivation Therapy on Affective Disorders," *Sleep Research,* Vol. 4 (Los Angeles: Brain Research Institute at University of California, 1975), p. 243.

Dunleavy, Yvonne, "How to Get Along on Less Sleep," *New York Sunday News,* June 8, 1975, pp. 18–19.

Edson, Lee, "Bad Day at the Office?", *Think,* July/August, 1977, pp. 30–33.

Evans, Frederick J., "Clinical Implications of Current Research in Sleep Disorders," draft of a paper presented at meeting "Psychiatric Update, 1978" at the Institute of Pennsylvania Hospital, Philadelphia, January 1978.

——, "Hypnosis and Sleep: The Control of Altered States of Awareness," *Annals of the New York Academy of Science,* Vol. 296 (October 7, 1977), pp. 162–74.

——, "Subjective Characteristics of Sleep Efficiency," *Journal of Abnormal Psychology,* Vol. 86 (October, 1977), pp. 561–64.

——, Mary Cook, Harvey Cohen, Emily Canota Orne, and Martin Orne, "Appetitive and Replacement Naps: EEG and Behavior," *Science,* Vol. 197 (August 12, 1977), pp. 687–89.

——, ——, ——, ——, and ——, "Sleep Patterns in Replacement and Appetitive Nappers," paper presented at the American Psychological Association, Washington, D.C., September, 1976.

Fincher, Jack, "Sleepers Are Given Polygraph Tests to Solve a Riddle," *Smithsonian,* November 1978, pp. 84–95.

Fishbein, Morris, "Solving the Mystery of Sleep," *Science Digest,* August 1967, pp. 43–44.

Flanagan, William, "How Much Sleep Do You Really

Need?", *Business Week,* August 31, 1974, pp. 69–70.

Foulkes, David, *The Psychology of Sleep.* New York: Charles Scribner's Sons, 1966.

——, "Sleep," *Encyclopedia Britannica,* 15th edition (Chicago: Encyclopedia Britannica, Inc., 1974), Vol. 16, pp. 876–83.

Friedmann, Joyce K., G. G. Globus, A. Huntley, D. J. Mullaney, P. Naitoh, and L. C. Johnson, "Performance and Mood During and After Gradual Sleep Reduction," *Psychophysiology,* Vol. 14 (May 1977), pp. 245–50.

Galvin, Ruth Mehrtens, "Probing the Mysteries of Sleep," *The Atlantic,* February 1979, pp. 53–61.

Gaylin, Jody, "The Way We Sleep Is the Way We Live," *Psychology Today,* May 1977, pp. 32–33.

"Getting Along with Getting Up," *Time,* February 14, 1969, p. 61.

"Getting Enough Sleep?", *Changing Times,* May 1968, p. 40.

Giles, Ray, *Sleep! The Secret of Greater Power and Achievement.* Indianapolis: The Bobbs-Merrill Company, 1938.

Globus, Gordon, "Sleep Duration and Feeling State," *International Psychiatry Clinics,* Vol. 7 (1970), pp. 78–84.

——, "A Syndrome Associated with Sleeping Late," *Psychosomatic Medicine,* Vol. 31 (1969), pp. 528–35.

Gove, Walter R., "Sleep Deprivation: A Cause of Psychotic Disorganization," *American Journal of Sociology,* Vol. 75 (March 1970), pp. 782–99.

Hackney, Ki, "Eating to Sleep," *American Home,* January 1976, p. 80.

Hall, Calvin S., and Robert L. Van de Castle, *The Content Analysis of Dreams.* New York: Appleton-Century-Crofts, 1966.

Hamilton, P., R. T. Wilkinson, and R. S. Edwards, "A

Study of Four Days of Partial Sleep Deprivation," in *Aspects of Human Efficiency: Diurnal Rhythm and Loss of Sleep,* ed. W. P. Colquhoun (London: The English Universities Press, Ltd., 1972), pp. 101–13.

Hammond, E. Cuyler, "Some Preliminary Findings on Physical Complaints from a Prospective Study of 1,064,004 Men and Women," *American Journal of Public Health,* Vol. 54 (January 1964), pp. 11–23.

——and Lawrence Garfinkel, "Coronary Heart Disease, Stroke and Aortic Aneurysm," *Archives of Environmental Health,* Vol. 19 (1969), pp. 167–82.

Hartmann, Ernest L., *The Functions of Sleep.* New Haven: Yale University Press, 1973.

——, "L-Tryptophan—The Sleeping Pill of the Future?", *Psychology Today,* December 1978, p. 180.

——, Frederick Baekeland, and George Zwilling, "Psychological Differences Between Long and Short Sleepers," *Archives of General Psychiatry,* Vol. 26 (May 1972), pp. 463–68.

——, ——, ——, and Patrick Hoy, "Sleep Need: How Much Sleep and What Kind?", *American Journal of Psychiatry,* Vol. 127 (February 1971), pp. 41–48.

Hauri, Peter, *The Sleep Disorders.* Kalamazoo, Mich.: The Upjohn Co., 1977.

Herman, John H., Steven J. Ellman, and Howard Roffwarg, "The Problem of NREM Dream Recall Reexamined," in *The Mind in Sleep: Psychology and Psychophysiology,* ed. A. Arkin, J. Antrobus and S. Ellman. Hillsdale, N.J.: Lawrence Erlbaum Associates, 1978.

Hicks, Robert A., and Robert J. Pellegrini, "Anxiety Levels of Short and Long Sleepers," *Psychological Reports,* Vol. 41 (1977), pp. 569–70.

Hobson, J. Allan, "Sleep After Exercise," *Science Digest,* December 27, 1968, pp. 1503–5.

Hoddes, Eric, "Does Sleep Help You Study?", *Psychology Today,* June 1977, p. 69.

——, V. Zarcone, H. Smythe, R. Phillips, and W. C.

Dement, "Quantification of Sleepiness: A New Approach," *Psychophysiology,* Vol. 10 (1973), pp. 431–36.

"How Much Sleep?", *Newsweek,* February 19, 1973, pp. 72–73.

"How Much Sleep Do You Need? Interview with Dr. Julius Segal, National Institute of Mental Health," *U.S. News & World Report,* December 28, 1970, pp. 30–34.

"How to Get a Night's Sleep, Interview with Dr. Elliot D. Weitzman, Director, Sleep Disorders Unit, Montefiore Hospital, New York City," *U.S. News & World Report,* August 8, 1977, pp. 62–64.

Johnson, Laverne C., "Are Stages of Sleep Related to Waking Behavior?", *American Scientist,* Vol. 61 (May–June, 1973), pp. 326–38.

——, "Psychological and Physiological Changes Following Total Sleep Deprivation," in *Sleep: Physiology & Pathology,* ed. Anthony Kales (Philadelphia: J. B. Lippincott Co., 1969), pp. 206–20.

—— and William L. MacLeod, "Sleep and Awake Behavior During Gradual Sleep Reduction," *Perceptual and Motor Skills,* Vol. 36 (1973), pp. 87–97.

——, Paul Naitoh, Ardie Lubin, and Julie Moses, "Sleep Stages and Performance," in *Aspects of Human Efficiency: Diurnal Rhythm and Loss of Sleep,* ed. W. P. Colquhoun (London: The English Universities Press, Ltd., 1972), pp. 81–99.

——, ——, ——, and ——, "Variations in Sleep Schedules," *Waking and Sleeping,* Vol. 1 (1977), pp. 133–37.

Jones, Henry S., and Ian Oswald, "Two Cases of Healthy Insomnia," *Electroencephalography and Clinical Neurophysiology,* Vol. 24 (1968), pp. 378–80.

Karacan, Ismet, Robert Williams, William Finley, and Carolyn Hursch, "The Effects of Naps on Nocturnal Sleep: Influence on the Need for Stage-1, REM and

Stage-4 Sleep," *Biological Psychiatry*, Vol. 2 (1970), pp. 391–99.

Kastner, Jonathan and Marianna, *Sleep: The Mysterious Third of Your Life*. New York: Harcourt, Brace & World, 1968.

Kjellberg, Anders, "Effects of Sleep Deprivation on Performance of a Problem-Solving Task," *Psychological Reports*, Vol. 37 (1975), pp. 479–85.

Kleban, Barbara, "Dr. Franz Halberg Measures the Body's Natural Cycles (But Please Don't Call Them Biorhythms)," *People*, November 6, 1978, pp. 123–25.

Kleitman, Nathaniel, "Basic Rest-Activity Cycle *(BRAC)*—Functioning of Nervous System," in *Sleep: Physiology & Pathology*, ed. Anthony Kales (Philadelphia: J. B. Lippincott Co., 1969), pp. 33–38.

——, *Sleep and Wakefulness*, revised edition. Chicago: University of Chicago Press, 1963.

——, F. J. Mullin, N. R. Cooperman, and S. Titelbaum, *Sleep Characteristics*. Chicago: University of Chicago Press, 1937.

Klemesrud, Judy, "Doesn't Anybody Here Count Sheep Any More?" *The New York Times*, November 3, 1971, p. 52.

Kripke, D. F., L. Garfinkel, E. C. Hammond, and R. N. Simons, "Average Sleep, Insomnia, and Sleeping Pill Use," *Sleep Research*, Vol. 5 (Los Angeles: Brain Research Institute of University of California, 1976), p. 110.

Lewis, Emma, "How to Get a Good Night's Sleep," *Harper's Bazaar*, September 1973, pp. 46, 69, 109.

Lewis, S. A., "Sleep Patterns During Afternoon Naps in the Young and Elderly," *British Journal of Psychiatry*, Vol. 115 (1969), pp. 107–8.

Lo Bello, Nino, "Italian Farmer Says He Has Not Slept for 20 Years, 'Travels' World," *Sacramento Bee*, October 12, 1970, n.p.

"Long vs. Short Sleepers," *Science Digest,* September 1972, p. 55.

Lubin, A., J. M. Moses, L. C. Johnson, and P. Naitoh, "The Recuperative Effects of REM Sleep and Stage 4 Sleep on Human Performance After Complete Sleep Loss: Experiment I," *Psychophysiology,* Vol. 11 (1974), pp. 133–46.

Lublin, Joann S., "Perchance to Dream: Sleep-Disorder Clinics Grow as Researchers Work Out Treatments," *The Wall Street Journal,* January 11, 1978, pp. 1, 23.

Luce, Gay Gaer, and Julius Segal, *Sleep.* New York: Coward-McCann, 1966.

——— and ———, "Sleep—From Alpha to Delta," *The New York Times Magazine,* April 17, 1966, pp. 28–29, 58–73.

——— and ———, "What Time Is It? The Body's Clock Knows," *The New York Times Magazine,* April 13, 1966, pp. 30, 120–24.

Masterton, J. P., "Sleep of Hospital Medical Staff," *The Lancet,* Vol. 1 (January 2, 1965), pp. 41–42.

Mattlin, Everett, "Executive Insomnia," *Town & Country,* February 1970, pp. 42–43.

Meddis, Ray, *The Sleep Instinct.* London: Routledge & Kegan Paul, 1977.

———, A. J. D. Pearson, and G. Langford, "An Extreme Case of Healthy Insomnia," *Electroencephalography and Clinical Neurophysiology,* Vol. 35 (1973), pp. 213–14.

"Meditation: Let's Sleep On It," *Science News,* Vol. 109 (January 24, 1976), p. 54.

Mitler, Merrill M., Christian Guilleminault, John Orem, Vincent Zarcone, and William Dement, "Sleeplessness, Sleep Attacks and Things That Go Wrong in the Night," *Psychology Today,* December 1975, pp. 45–50.

Moses, Julie M., L. C. Johnson, P. Naitoh, and A. Lubin, "Sleep Stage Deprivation and Total Sleep

Loss: Effects on Sleep Behavior," *Psychophysiology,* Vol. 12 (1975), pp. 141–46.

Mullaney, D. J., L. C. Johnson, P. Naitoh, J. K. Friedmann, and G. G. Globus, "Sleep During and After Gradual Sleep Reduction," *Psychophysiology,* Vol. 14 (May 1977), pp. 237–44.

"NASA-developed Sleep Analyzer," *Space World,* Vol. H–10–94 (October 1971), p. 41.

"The Natural Ways to Get to Sleep," *Harper's Bazaar,* October 1974, p. 84.

Nolen, William A., "How to Sleep," *McCall's,* October 1973, pp. 52–54, 150.

Oddo, Sandra, "Do Patterned Sheets Soothe Your Psyche?", *House & Garden,* September 1975, pp. 64, 135.

Ogilvie, Robert, and Sidney Segalowitz, "The Effect of 20% Sleep Reduction Upon Mood, Learning and Performance Measures," *Sleep Research,* Vol. 4 (Los Angeles: Brain Research Institute of University of California, 1975), p. 242.

Oswald, Ian, *Sleeping and Waking.* Amsterdam, N.Y.: Elsevier Publishing Co., 1962.

Pagano, Robert R., Richard Rose, Robert Stivers, and Stephen Warrenburg, "Sleep During Transcendental Meditation," *Science,* Vol. 191 (January 1976), pp. 308–10.

Pasnau, Robert O., Paul Naitoh, Serena Stier, and Edward J. Kollar, "The Psychological Effects of 205 Hours of Sleep Deprivation," *Archives of General Psychiatry,* Vol. 18 (April 1968), pp. 496–505.

Pembrook, Linda, "The Wonderful Wonder Drug: Sleep," *Cosmopolitan,* September 1977, pp. 199–203.

"Pillow Talk," *Time,* July 3, 1978, p. 23.

Ratcliff, J. D., "Are You Getting Enough Sleep?", *Reader's Digest,* May 1967, pp. 109–11.

"Report on Sleep Research," *Science Digest,* June 1971, pp. 58–59.

"Retired Italian Farmer Stays Awake 30 Years," *GRIT,* July 10, 1977, n.p.

Rodgers, Joann Ellison, "How to Get a Good Night's Sleep," *Ladies' Home Journal,* March 1979, pp. 86–91.

Roesch, Roberta, "Ten Tips for Getting Out of Bed in the Morning," *Family Health,* November 1976, pp. 42–43.

Russell, Beverly, "Sleep: An Interview with Elliot Weitzman," *House & Garden,* April 1973, pp. 124–25, 146–47.

"The Salutary Seven," *Fortune,* February 1977, p. 169.

Sanford, Kay, "To Sleep . . . Perchance to Dream," *Science Digest,* April 1978, pp. 11–12, 16.

Scarf, Maggie, "Oh, for a Decent Night's Sleep!", *The New York Times Magazine,* October 21, 1973, pp. 70–71, 79–82. (Included in Scarf, *Body, Mind, Behavior.* New York: Dell Publishing Company, 1976, pp. 90–106.)

Schmeck, Harold M., Jr., "U.S. Study of Sleep Drugs Finds Risks and Overuse," *The New York Times,* April 5, 1979, pp. 1, A18.

Schwartz, Alice K., and Norma S. Aaron, "The Quest of Sleep," *New York,* February 26, 1979, pp. 45–52.

Seebohm, Caroline, "The Secrets of a Good Night's Sleep," *House & Garden,* August 1975, p. 132.

——,"Taking a Nap: What It Can Do for You," *House & Garden,* February 1977, pp. 26, 137.

——, "What to Do to Guarantee a Good Night's Sleep," *House & Garden,* August 1975, p. 46, 132.

Segal, Julius, "How Do You Feel After Sex—Sleepy or Exhilarated? You May Be Fooling Yourself," *Glamour,* May 1978, pp. 78, 86.

Shapiro, Jane, "New Reasons to Pay Attention to Your Dreams," *Mademoiselle,* February 1979, pp. 154–55, 202–3.

"Sleep and Emotions," *Time,* June 29, 1970, p. 53.

Sleep and the Sleep Disorders: A New Clinical Discipline, symposium for science and health writers sponsored by the Albert Einstein College of Medicine; Sleep-Wake Disorders Unit of the Department of Neurology, Montefiore Hospital and Medical Center; and The Upjohn Company; New York, December 1976.

"Sleep Clinic's Experts Say Most Older People Need Less Sleep Than Younger Adults," *Retirement Living,* February 1977, pp. 11–12.

"Sleep for the Memory," *Time,* August 23, 1976, p. 39.

"Sleep: How to Get More Out of Less," *Mademoiselle,* August 1969, pp. 283, 383–84.

"Sleep, Perchance to REM," *Newsweek,* May 23, 1966, p. 104.

"Sleep: Problems and Remedies," *Mademoiselle,* April 1975, p. 139.

"Sleep: You Can't Live Without It," *Redbook,* January 1977, p. 62.

"Sleeping Easy," *Scientific American,* May 1969, p. 54.

Snider, Arthur J., "Light Sleepers More Active than Long Sleepers," *Science Digest,* September 1970, p. 81.

Snyder, Frederick, J. Allan Hobson, Donald F. Morrison, and Frederick Goldfrank, "Changes in Respiration, Heart Rate, and Systolic Blood Pressure in Human Sleep," in *Sleep: An Active Process,* ed. Wilse B. Webb. Glenview, Ill.: Scott, Foresman and Co., 1973, pp. 85–100.

Spinweber, Cheryl, and Ernest Hartmann, "Long and Short Sleepers: Male and Female Subjects," *Sleep Research,* Vol. 5 (Los Angeles: Brain Research Institute of University of California, 1976), p. 112.

Stuss, Donald, Thomas Healey, and Roger Broughton, "Personality and Performance Measures in Natural Extreme Short Sleepers," *Sleep Research,* Vol. 4 (Los Angeles: Brain Research Institute of University of California, 1975), p. 204.

"Surviving Without Sleep," *The New York Times Magazine,* November 11, 1973, pp. 35, 59.

Switzer, Ellen, "Sleep Myths Exploded," *Vogue,* February 15, 1972, pp. 48–49.

—— and George Langmyhr, "Your Sex Life and How It Affects the Way You Sleep," *Vogue,* August 1973, pp. 120–21, 148.

Talmey, Allene, "What You Must Know About Your Sleep and Dreams," *Vogue,* November 15, 1968, pp. 166–67.

Taub, John M., and Ralph J. Berger, "Acute Shifts in Sleep-Wakefulness Cycle: Effects on Performance and Mood," *Psychosomatic Medicine,* Vol. 36 (March-April 1974), pp. 164–73.

—— and ——, "The Effects of Changing the Phase and Duration of Sleep," *Journal of Experimental Psychology,* Vol. 7 (1976), pp. 30–41.

—— and ——, "Performance and Mood Following Variations in the Length and Timing of Sleep," *Psychophysiology,* Vol. 10 (1973), pp. 559–70.

——, Peter Tanguay, and Douglas Clarkson, "Effects of Daytime Naps on Performance and Mood in a College Student Population," *Journal of Abnormal Psychology,* Vol. 85 (1976), pp. 210–17.

"Time-Zone Trauma: Every Traveler Has a Therapy for Jet Lag, But Malady Lingers," *The Wall Street Journal,* March 7, 1978, pp. 1, 41.

"Too Much Sleep?", *Time,* October 25, 1968, p. 64.

Trubo, Richard, "The Complete Sleep Book," *Good Housekeeping,* March 1978, pp. 77–80, 274–82.

"The Truth About Sleep," *Mademoiselle,* March 1977, p. 98.

Vogel, Gerald W., "REM Deprivation: Dreaming and Psychosis," *Archives of General Psychiatry,* Vol. 18 (March 1968), pp. 312–29.

"Wake Up from These Sleep Myths," *Good Housekeeping,* May 1972, p. 209.

Wallace, Robert Keith, Robert R. Pagano, Richard M.

Rose, and Stephen Warrenburg, "TM: Meditation or Sleep?", *Science,* Vol. 193 (August 27, 1976), pp. 719–20.

Webb, Wilse B., "Did Edison Invent Non-Sleep, Too?" *Sleep Forum* ("letter" issued by the Department of Psychiatry, University of Texas, Dallas), 1978, pp. 25–27.

——, "Doing What Comes Naturally: A Review of Ray Meddis' *The Sleep Instinct,*" *Contemporary Psychology,* Vol. 23 (1978), p. 399.

——, "On Sleep: The Long and the Short of It," *The New York Times,* August 22, 1975, p. 31.

——, "Partial and Differential Sleep Deprivation," in *Sleep: Physiology & Pathology,* ed. Anthony Kales (Philadelphia: J. B. Lippincott Co., 1969), pp. 221–31.

——, "Patterns of Sleep Behavior," in *Aspects of Human Efficiency: Diurnal Rhythm and Loss of Sleep,* ed. W. P. Colquhoun (London: The English Universities Press, Ltd., 1972), pp. 31–46.

——, "Sleep As An Adaptive Response," *Perceptual and Motor Skills,* Vol. 38 (1974), pp. 1023–27.

——, *Sleep: The Gentle Tyrant.* Englewood Cliffs, N.J.: Prentice-Hall, 1975.

——, "Twenty-Four-Hour Sleep Cycling," in *Sleep: Physiology & Pathology,* ed. Anthony Kales (Philadelphia: J. B. Lippincott Co., 1969), pp. 53–65.

—— and H. W. Agnew, Jr., "Are We Chronically Sleep Deprived?", *Bulletin of the Psychonomic Society,* Vol. 6 (1975), pp. 47–48.

—— and ——, "The Effects of a Chronic Limitation of Sleep Length," *Psychophysiology,* Vol. 11 (1974), pp. 265–74.

—— and ——, "Effects on Performance of High and Low Energy-Expenditure During Sleep Deprivation," *Perceptual and Motor Skills,* Vol. 37 (1973), pp. 511–14.

—— and ——, "The Effects on Subsequent Sleep of

an Acute Restriction of Sleep Length," *Psychophysiology,* Vol. 12 (1975), pp. 367–70.

—— and ——, "Sleep: Effect of a Restricted Regime," *Science,* Vol. 150 (December 1965), pp. 1765–66.

—— and ——, "Sleep Stage Characteristics of Long and Short Sleepers," *Science,* Vol. 168 (April 8, 1970), pp. 146–47.

——, Michael Bonnet, and Royce White, "State and Trait Correlates of Sleep Stages," *Psychological Reports,* Vol. 38 (1976), pp. 1181–82.

—— and Janette Friel, "Sleep Stage and Personality Characteristics of 'Natural' Long and Short Sleepers," *Science,* Vol. 171 (February 12, 1971), pp. 587–88.

"What Scientists Really Know About Sleep," *Good Housekeeping,* February 1966, p. 161.

"What's in a Dream," *Newsweek,* January 16, 1978, p. 50.

Wilkinson, R. T., "Sleep Deprivation—Eight Questions," in *Aspects of Human Efficiency: Diurnal Rhythm and Loss of Sleep,* ed. W. P. Colquhoun (London: The English Universities Press, Ltd., 1972), pp. 25–30.

Williams, Harold L., Ardie Lubin, and Jacqueline J. Goodnow, "Impaired Performance with Acute Sleep Loss," *Psychological Monographs: General and Applied,* No. 484 (1959).

Young, Patrick, "Dreams Set Your Mood," *The National Observer,* June 20, 1977, pp. 1, 13.

——, "To Sleep, Perchance to Dream . . .", *American Way,* April 1978, pp. 38–43.

Young, Warren, "Five Rules for Waking Up Alert," *Reader's Digest,* June 1972, pp. 217–18.

INDEX